SHELTON STATE COMMUNITY COLLEGE
JUNIOR COLLEGE DIVISION
LIBRARY

DISCARDED

W9-BND-023

HD
3850   Sharkansky, Ira
.S45
           Wither the state?

DATE DUE			

Other books by Ira Sharkansky:

Spending in the American States
The Politics of Taxing and Spending
Regionalism in American Politics
The Routines of Politics
Public Administration: Policy-Making in Government Agencies
Policy Analysis in Political Science
State and Urban Politics (with Richard I. Hofferbert)
Urban Politics and Public Policy (with Robert L. Lineberry)
The Maligned States: Policy Accomplishments, Problems, and Opportunities
Policy and Politics in American Governments (with Donald S. Van Meter)
The United States: A Study of a Developing Country
The Policy Predicament: Making and Implementing Public Policy
    (with George C. Edwards III)

WITHER THE STATE?

Politics and Public Enterprise
in Three Countries

Ira Sharkansky

CHATHAM HOUSE PUBLISHERS, INC.
CHATHAM, NEW JERSEY

WITHER THE STATE?
Politics and Public Enterprise in Three Countries

CHATHAM HOUSE PUBLISHERS, INC.
Post Office Box One
Chatham, New Jersey 07928

Copyright ©1979 by Chatham House Publishers, Inc.

All rights reserved. No part of this publication may be reproduced, stored in a retrieval system or transmitted in any form or by any means, electronic, mechanical, photocopying, recording, or otherwise, without the prior permission of the publisher.

Executive Editor: Edward Artinian
Interior Design: Pencils Portfolio, Inc.
Exterior Design: Lawrence Ratzkin
Composition: Columbia Publishing Company, Inc.
Printing and Binding: Hamilton Printing Company

Library of Congress Cataloging in Publication Data
    Sharkansky, Ira
        Wither the state?

        Includes bibliographical references and index.
        1. Government business enterprises — Australia.
    2. Government business enterprises — Israel.
    3. Government business enterprises — United States.
    4. Welfare state — Case studies. I. Title.
    HD3850.S45   350'.0092   79-18780
    ISBN 0-934540-01-2
    ISBN 0-934540-00-4 pbk.

Manufactured in the United States of America

10 9 8 7 6 5 4 3 2 1

For Erica and Stefan

Contents

Preface

This is a statement of conditions that appear generally in modern states and a study of public enterprise in three countries. Modern states are both growing and withering. They grow in response to incessant demands for more services; they wither as officials assign important activities to bodies that enjoy formal grants of autonomy from the state. Enter public enterprise. The character of the enterprise varies with the setting. A country's political culture, government structure, and economy shape the form and practice of its public enterprise. There is something typically Australian about that country's statutory authorities, just as there is something typically Israeli about that country's government companies and something typically American about the special authorities and government contractors of the United States.

The importance of this topic to political scientists, and to citizens generally, derives from the large roles being played by public enterprises located on the margins of the modern state. In many countries, activities on the margins of the state have grown larger than activities performed by core departments of government. Matters of great importance — planning, implementing and evaluating social services, industrial activity, energy, transport, and finance — come from organizations that operate with the powers and resources of the state, but without those controls that are supposed to link the public with public servants.

There is much good work and no few problems on the margins of the state. The problems occur as much in the work of political scientists as in public administration. Information about the margins of the state does not match the magnitude of the activities performed there. If this book is successful, more political scientists will turn their attention to the margins of the state and will seek to understand them as well as they have come to understand the conventional mechanisms of elections, legislatures, chief executives, and government departments.

This book owes much to my good fortune. Faculty appointments at The Hebrew University of Jerusalem, The University of Wisconsin-Madison, and Monash University in the suburbs of Melbourne offered me opportunities to work in Israeli, American, and Australian settings. I hesitate to thank colleagues by name in each of these universities in order to avoid slighting, unintentionally, any of the many who were helpful. Colleagues from other universities in each of these countries were generous with their time and their ideas. Ronald Webster of Victoria's Treasury and Benjamin Geist of the Israeli State Comptroller have been helpful as guides to their governments and as critics. Professor John Roberts of the Victoria University in Wellington, New Zealand, was a gracious host and arranged valuable contacts in his country; the same was true of Professor Francesco Kjellberg of the University of Oslo. Professor Richard Rose introduced me into his European group on overloaded government. Each of these people was invaluable in guiding me both to the universality and the particularity of the Australian, Israeli, and American cases. At the Hebrew University Shlomo Greenberg was a tireless and productive research assistant, as was Robert X. Browning at the University of Wisconsin. I owe great thanks to all these people, and to others. I also want to thank the three universities in which I have held appointments, for their support services, and the Ford Foundation-Israel and the Graduate Research Committee of the University of Wisconsin, for research funds.

My children, Erica and Stefan, deserve this dedication. They have been loyal and loving, and always loved.

WITHER THE STATE?

1

THE INCOHERENCE OF WELFARE STATES

The state grows, but it also declines. It does more while doing less. It confounds those who would understand and control it, while it adds to the benefits offered to its citizens. The nature of the state changes. Observers are unable to describe its activities or measure its size. State officials will not, or cannot, report the true size of the budget or the work force. The modern state defies definition. And because they cannot say exactly what it is, participants in the state have as many problems controlling it as observers have describing it. Both politicians and political scientists suffer from confusion about the thing that is central to their careers.

The blurring of the state is partly a matter of deception and partly a matter of coping with demands that run counter to one another. There are great pressures on politicians to offer more services without increasing taxes and without increasing the work force. Politicians, who already have difficulty supervising the far-flung departments of government, seek to avoid additional departments and more employees. How to do more with less is a central question of the welfare state. It is possible to do more while seeming to do less, at least in the short run and with narrow definitions of the state's responsibilities. This is a political shell game. A clear understanding of the state suffers in the illusion of doing more with less.

States do more while they do less by assigning activities to corporate bodies that are not, strictly speaking, part of the state. Just how this happens depends on conditions within each country. For example, from 1955 to 1976 the federal government of the United States has, in certain respects, actually become smaller in size. The number of U.S. federal employees declined from 146 per 10,000 population to 134 per 10,000 population. Yet no one could claim that the federal government did less in 1976 than it did in 1955. It shrunk by assigning elsewhere new activities and some old established programs. Washington transferred some activities to state and local governments; it assigned others to private firms or foundations operating as contractors for government agencies.

The inclination to use business firms or other private units as government contractors is distinctly an American style of conducting public activities outside the borders of the state. By tradition the United States is a country of free enterprise. It is fitting to use business corporations to implement many of the programs that have turned the United States into one of the most generous of welfare states.

In other countries there is less preoccupation with free enterprise, and less tendency to assign the state's activities to private business. The more common pattern in wealthy Western societies is to assign responsibilities to government-owned companies or to special authorities created by acts of the legislature. Such special authorities also exist in the United States, and there are some U.S. companies owned by the government. As in the case of firms operating under contract to the government, these government companies or special authorities are distinct from the state even while they are doing the state's business. Typically the employees of government-owned companies or special authorities—like the employees of private firms under contract to American governments—are not considered state employees. The revenues and expenditures of these bodies are not included in the state's budget. Usually there is no central listing of government-owned companies, special authorities, or government contractors. These entities exist in a gray area on the margins of the state. Because they are big and important, they create problems for officials of the state, for clients who would receive their services, and for political scientists who would understand their policies.

There have long been creatures on the margins of the state. The United States has relied on government contractors since the Revolutionary War. And since then it has suffered from firms that did not deliver the goods promised, or delivered goods of shoddy quality or at exorbitant prices. In like manner, for many years there have been special authorities with responsibilities to construct public works and run public utilities. Governments have long found themselves owning companies, either by design or when private firms defaulted on their obligations and surrendered their assets to a government office.

Now the margins of some states have grown larger than government itself. The size of these creatures warrants renewed attention. Because they are largely self-governing, these bodies have, in their growth, threatened some of political science with obsolescence. Concerns about elections, legislatures, chief executives, and government departments have limited appeal if governments isolate most of what they do from these devices of political control.

There is some conjecture in the statement that the margins of the state are larger than its core. Estimates are necessary because the margins are so little examined. They come in for scant attention by official records of "governmental" activity. Most political scientists and journalists focus on the conventional institutions of the state and ignore the margins.

One estimate out of Washington is that more people work for private firms under contract to the U.S. government than work for the government directly. More precise estimates dealing with the Department of Health, Education, and Welfare — one of the most active civilian users of government contractors — is that 750,000 people work under contract to HEW, whereas only 157,000 are employees of HEW. Again it is necessary to stress the vagueness of these figures. Not only are they estimates of no clear certainty but they do not allow any equation of a government employee with a contractor's employee. Many of the contractors' employees may work only part-time on projects for HEW. In other words, the estimates are not offered as "full-time equivalents."

Other information suggests that special authorities may have grown larger in some respects than the governments associated with them. Special authorities attached to American states and localities are said to borrow more than all state and local governments combined. Special authorities spend some $10 billion a year on new facilities. By way of comparison, California and New York spent $983 million and $1.8 billion on capital projects in 1974.[1]

The State of Israel acknowledges that it owns a majority of the stock in 105 companies, according to the 1976-77 report of its Government Companies Authority. There is no central listing of those companies in which the government owns less than 50 percent of the stock, the subsidiary companies owned by the 105 government-owned companies, or the joint ventures held partly by government-owned companies and partly by other investors. The civil servants of Israel and the officers of government-owned companies show the entrepreneurialism to be expected from employees of the Jewish state. They have been aggressive and imaginative in creating subsidiaries and partnerships. A result is that government leaders do not know what they own, or what they might try to control.

The leaders of Israel's Labor Federation, the Histadrut, are also in the dark. The Histadrut has been developing companies since the 1920s. It has acquired a role in every sector of the economy, and owns or participates as a shareholder in the largest companies of Israel. When the government and the Histadrut seek partners, they usually find one another. One estimate has the Histadrut as whole or part owner of 2000 companies.[2] The roundness of the number does not encourage confidence in its accuracy.

The State of Victoria, in southeastern Australia, claims to have made an important contribution to the development of bodies marginal to the state. A common variety of such bodies, statutory authorities, began with the creation of Victorian Railways in 1856. Today statutory authorities provide banking, energy, transportation, town planning, housing, and a host of other services throughout Australia. There appears to be no single list of Commonwealth of Australia plus state government authorities.

Nevertheless, in keeping with the orderliness of Australians, they can produce better estimates about the size of their margins than can the other governments in this study. The Public Service Board of Victoria notes that core departments of the state government employ about one sixth the number of persons attached to the statutory authorities of the state. This means that the Public Service Board, which supposedly monitors and controls the state's public servants, is responsible for only 16 percent of the larger concept of the public sector that includes the state and its margins.

British observers use the acronym QUANGO for bodies on the margins of their state. The term stands for "quasi-autonomous government organization." Critics estimated that about 900 QUANGOs make available some 8000 paid and 25,000 unpaid appointments, which might be filled outside the framework of conventional civil service procedures.[3]

A UNIVERSAL PROBLEM
WITH NATIONAL VARIANTS

The proliferation of governmental activities on the margins of the state seems to be a universal trait. At the heart of the matter is the public demand for governmental activity, which results in so many programs that they spill beyond what government officials can control. This can be summarized in a bold sentence that will require some discussion: *All modern states are welfare states, and all welfare states are incoherent.*

This contentious statement begs definitions. In fact, "modern states," "welfare states," and "incoherence" can only be clarified. Their semantic and ideological connotations defy definitions that will escape the charge "that is not what the word *really* means."

In a "welfare state," the government or its agents provide a wide range of social services. Individuals are not left on their own to go hungry, unclothed, ignorant, unhoused, or to suffer the ravages of disease without care. Powerful individuals or firms cannot seek profit without regulation.

"Welfare" is a term that goes beyond its use in American politics. To many Americans, "welfare" means income support, or public assistance, or what Australians call the "dole." As used in this book, however, "welfare" refers to the full range of social programs and regulatory powers assumed by modern states. Included in the programs of a welfare state are income support, schooling, health care, housing, economic stability, environmental protection, and the monitoring of business practices. A welfare state assumes responsibility to enhance opportunities for jobs, to protect citizens against inflation, and to guard the national economy from problems originating beyond its borders. Welfare states differ, to be sure, in the extent and manner in which they provide services or regulate private behavior. The problem of definition is made no easier by the universality of welfare states. There may be no nonwelfare modern states available for comparison. It is possible to discern a nonwelfare state in the fantasies of certain Republicans and others farther to the right in the United States, but their references are to the dim past of the 1920s.

A "modern state" is one based on a well-developed economy, and with a certain degree of political stability. Democracy is not a prerequisite. A certain level of resources and a certain level of administrative capacity are important, however, in assuring that the services promised in legislation are actually delivered, more or less, to the population.

Not counted among modern welfare states are many poor countries whose constitutions or laws promise a full range of education, health services, and pensions but whose economies lack the wherewithal to make such programs widely available.

What modern states are also welfare states? All but the poorest European countries qualify, both East and West. Included, too, are Canada and the United States, as well as Japan, Israel, Singapore, Australia, and New Zealand. Such a list is meant to be illustrative more than exhaustive. Omissions should not be viewed as condemnations. Some omissions reflect an uncertainty as to how well delivered are the country's promises of social services.

"Incoherence" is another loaded term. It sounds bad. Perhaps it means that welfare states are bad states? Not at all. "Incoherence" is descriptive. It is meant not to condemn but to portray a common feature of modern welfare states. If being a welfare state and being incoherent are inevitable for modern states, there is little point in condemnation.

"Incoherence" means a lack of understandability. Modern welfare states are so complicated that people who should be able to know what is going on cannot do so. There is something about being a welfare state that assures complexity to the point of incoherence. Popular demands for extensive services cause public agencies to proliferate. There may be a way of organizing to assure coherence in the eyes of officials or citizens, but no one has succeeded in doing this. The assignment of units to the margins of the state may create an illusion of tight control over the core departments of the government. However, the bits that are simple and neatly arrayed in government departments are becoming a smaller percentage of what the government is really doing.

There are different aspects of incoherence, each with its implications for clients, politicians, and other government officials. One aspect of incoherence is a lack of manageability. By this I mean that different phases of related processes cannot be fitted together because of administrative snafus. Classic are the cases of Soviet industry that produce too many of some components but not enough of others. Partly finished tractors clog the final assembly plant because of shortages in engines, wheels, or axles.

The different pieces of social programs also must come together. More than 330 separate programs funnel out from the U.S. Department of Health, Education, and Welfare to states and localities. Different offices handle activities that must be assembled together for effective delivery, such as counseling plus training and job placement. Many clients lack the ability to figure out the system and go after what they need. Interoffice hostility and sheer ignorance on the part of bureaucrats stifle effective referrals. There is a high incidence of clients visiting the wrong offices and being sent elsewhere.

Incoherence deters political accountability. Elected members of the legislature cannot supervise important features of the public's business because they cannot learn who is responsible for what, or how to bring about desired changes in programs. Often problems of accountability arise because legislators earlier encouraged the transfer of activities to contractors or special authorities, and gave assurance of "autonomy" to these bodies as protection against "political interference." Yet some degree of "political interference" is essential to political accountability. How can legislators represent the people if they cannot probe the public's business?

The aimless pursuit of a responsive clerk is a part of modern life. A politician can help a citizen by adding the prestige of office to the quest. This is political accountability at the street level. If the errant clerk works for a special authority or a government contractor, however, there are added problems for both the client and the politician. The legislature may lack the clout of budget approval over a special authority. A private company that collects garbage may have an assured monopoly over the life of a contract, with no competition waiting in the wings. It takes a lot of money to buy the equipment needed for such a task. Once a community decides to contract-out trash collection, it may find itself stuck with one contractor and little control over its services.

The diversity that comes with numerous autonomous bodies means that records are kept in peculiar ways, according to no common format. Information sought by politicians in order to help constituents may be available in raw form but capable of assemblage only at great expense. The Wisconsin Department of Administration headed off one legislative request for information about government contractors by asserting that it would require examination of 1.5 million documents!

Problems of incoherence also surface in foreign policy. When the colony of Rhodesia broke away from Great Britain and declared its independence, Britain joined other nations in declaring an economic boycott. Some years later it became apparent that Rhodesia continued to receive substantial oil supplies from British Petroleum, one of the companies on the margin of the British state. British government officials claimed that the company took advantage of complex dealings with intermediaries to keep its trade with Rhodesia hidden from its governmental masters. At a certain point the government seemed to learn what was happening and then let it continue in the hope that others would also fail to notice.

Democracy is not essential to incoherence. The free play of interests in well-to-do countries of the West may aggravate tendencies toward incoherence. With more groups actively demanding programs, there may be a higher probability of more service providers, and more confused lines of authority. Yet the problem also occurs in the regimented states of Eastern Europe.

Principal actors in Soviet urban politics are officers of various ministries, the Communist party, and government enterprises. Local members of these bureaucracies depend on higher levels of their own organizations; there is no coordination at the local level. If the local party or government wishes to change the policies of industry, it must convince higher-echelon industry, party, and government officers to change programs at the top of the industry's hierarchy. Such an action may require extensive reconsideration of nationwide priorities. The spillovers of such decisions can affect economic planning for other locales whose industries would be affected by requested changes. In such exercises, there emerges the weight of the multiple bureaucracies that are both the mechanisms and the problems of Soviet policy making.

In concrete terms, such problems stand in the way of Soviet local government and party personnel altering the activities of local enterprises that create serious problems. Housing, mass transportation, and other services lag behind the creation of industry. Such services may be under the control of factory managers expected to provide amenities for their employees but rewarded by their superiors for industrial production. The Soviet system has struggled to change the orientation of factory managers from quantity to quality of production, and now it is struggling to develop some concern for the quality of life in the locales that surround the factories.[4]

The Soviet Union does not present the only case of incoherence among the regimes of Eastern Europe. A Polish expert summarizes local decision making in words that seem nearly universal:

Everyone who has examined local power in Poland knows the difficulties encountered in obtaining information, or sometimes even the impossibility of getting answers to questions concerning roles in the decision process. In my opinion, the context . . . in which the majority of local decisions are made creates the situation in which the process seems unclear, even to the actors.[5]

WHAT ARE WE DOING?

The principal concern of this book is with the *margins* of the modern state and their relations with the *core departments of government*. These terms also defy precise definition. Details and terminology differ from one country to another. In general, core departments are those featured on a government's organization chart, directly responsible to the head of state through ministers or department heads. Their employees are members of the civil service, and their expenditures appear in the government's budget. On the margins of the state are those bodies related to the core departments but with substantial grants of autonomy from them. The margins include some units clearly attached to the government (e.g., the statutory authorities of Australia) even when they hire staff outside the framework of civil service and enjoy substantial grants of financial and managerial autonomy. Other bodies on the margins of the state may be responsive to both state and nonstate masters (e.g., the Israeli companies owned partly by the government and partly by other investors). Still other marginal bodies may be described as "entirely" private (e.g., companies that contract with American governments). Even these "private" companies design or deliver important features of government policy and serve as extensions or surrogates, albeit somewhat autonomous ones, of core departments.

WHY PUT ORGANIZATIONS
ON THE MARGINS?

Sometimes government officials put units on the margins of their state because they cannot supervise all the programs that citizens demand. Politicians also see an opportunity for themselves on the margins. They can assign a risky venture to the margins and call it independent. If it fails, the politicians consider themselves free of blame. If it succeeds, they can claim credit. In politics as in war, victory knows many parents; defeat is an orphan.

Patronage is another reason for assigning programs to the margins of the state. Insofar as special authorities or companies escape the rules designed to curb favoritism in government departments, a politician can use them to take special care of friends, past supporters, or family members. Units on the margin of the state can provide sinecures for civil servants who should be kicked upstairs. They also provide funds outside the state budget for special projects that might not win legislative approval.

Patronage is a morally neutral way of describing things that politicians do for their own reasons without going through the rigmarole of red tape. Some patronage is clearly self-centered and done at the public's expense; the appointment of incompetent relatives or campaign supporters to positions in a government company fits into this category. Yet other patronage is more public in its orientation. Programs on the margins of the state can be tailor-made to serve a particular region or community, whereas core departments of the government may be required to provide equivalent services for the whole population. Such general requirements may lessen the government's ability to meet the particular needs of one community, or make the services prohibitively expensive because they must be given to the entire population. Chapter 3 describes one activity on the margin of the State of Israel that seeks to meet the special needs of the Old City in Jerusalem for a community television antenna. On a much larger scale, a body on the margin of the Italian state seeks to promote economic development in the southern region of that country.

Some developments may occur on the margins of a state because officials genuinely believe in principles of managerial autonomy. Certainly a great deal of rhetoric seeks to justify important assignments to bodies largely independent of government supervision and control. People express their views in behalf of managers in government-owned companies, special authorities, or private firms doing business with the government. They refer to matters that should be decided without detailed participation by government officials, in order to take advantage of the speed or expertise believed to exist in the private sector. It is always difficult to discern the genuine motives in such language. Discussions of principle may be only window dressing for patronage or the inability to encompass a new program in an established department of government. Although it is possible to list in the abstract numerous reasons for putting activities on the margins of the state, it is seldom possible to say with certainty precisely *why* a particular activity was put on the margins and not in a core department.

IMPLICATIONS OF GROWTH ON THE MARGINS OF THE STATE

The universality of incoherent welfare states makes for a certain dullness of analysis. If all modern states are incoherent welfare states, is there any more to say? Yes. First, bloated margins of the state and incoherence differ from place to place. Later chapters will show that national differences occur in keeping with underlying traits of culture, economics, and government. Second, the implications of bloated margins and incoherence touch many features of politics, government, and public policies. They are important features of our lives, and we can benefit from a full explication of how they appear and how they touch us.

Failures in Accountability

Accountability is the key to orderly government. It links the various organs of administration to the officials charged with defining public policy. If a government claims to be democratic, accountability ties the administration to key elected officials and thereby gives to the electorate some control over their government. For accountability to work in practice, top officials must be able to supervise and control what goes on in all organs of the government. Yet the growth of important functions on the margins of the state signifies the inability of elected officials to govern all they have created. Government ministers of the six states in Australia have all but given up formal control over the statutory authorities. One minister has a department of only 9 persons — including file clerks and stenographers — to aid him in supervising statutory authorities having close to 20,000 employees. Another minister, in charge of overseeing authorities with over 30,000 employees that touch the lives of every resident in his state, allows the heads of two major authorities to deal with him directly, without going through key professionals in the ministry. This minister thereby squanders his potential for checking proposals of the authorities against independent advice.

It is not only key elected officials who have surrendered authority to the margins of the state. Major appointed personnel, who nominally aid the elected branches in controlling the bureaucracy, also permit much activity to go unmonitored. Like the politicians, they may be giving in to the inevitable growth of public activities beyond the supervisory capacity of conventional government.

Snafus in Management
and Service Delivery

What difference does it make for programs when more and more of governments' work is done on the margins of the state? There is no clear answer at this point. Remember, government officials and political scientists have little information about these bodies. Nevertheless, what information does exist is enough to fill at least a small chamber of horrors. If it is not certain that the most serious problems come from the margins of the state, it is true that *some very serious* problems occur there. In September-October of 1977 the State Electricity Commission (SEC) of Victoria came to a crisis point as a result of a strike by maintenance personnel. The commission kept key officials of the state government informed of the situation, but the political leaders did not involve themselves directly until the commission took draconian action. The SEC rationed electricity in order to conserve power from those generators still operating. No electricity was available for industry, and some half a million workers were without jobs for four weeks.

No observer of Israeli affairs would argue that government companies produce the most important problems of that society. A history filled with war and economic constraint preoccupies Israeli citizens and officials. Nevertheless, the problems of government companies add their fillip of inconvenience. Frequent strikes at the national airline and shipping company cause delay and economic loss to travelers and business firms. Government companies that build housing and government mortgage banks cause large numbers of complaints to the ombudsman. The margins of the Israeli government are broad enough to include the Histadrut's Sick Fund, whose personnel, clinics, and hospitals serve three quarters of the population. The Sick Fund stirs countless complaints about oppressive procedures and unresponsive clerks. Moreover, a recent director of the Sick Fund is now sitting in prison for taking undue personal advantage of the blurred lines of control.

Shrill complaints about waste, mismanagement, and fraud also surround contractors that design or deliver social services for government agencies in the United States. Groups that oppose contracting include Ralph Nader's Center for the Study of Responsive Laws and the American Federation of State, County, and Municipal Employees. They document contracts awarded for reasons of political party patronage or nepotism; contracts for studies or services that produce neither; contracts that present a cost-saving image but are really more costly than activities provided by government departments; and the entry of organized crime into government contracting.[6]

Contracting adds to the offices involved in providing a service and multiplies problems of coordination. The U.S. government is said to employ 80,000 persons in order to supervise contracts. The Defense Department alone recorded more than 10 million contracts in one recent year. Complaints to government officials about contractors bring counterclaims about the contractor's autonomy and threaten a client with a lengthy and cumbersome struggle. Many governments have put key features of their social programs in the hands of the private sector. Government employees' claims under their health insurance may be processed by a private company, most likely by a division of the H. Ross Perot business empire that has sold its services throughout the country. A great deal of subsidized health care to needy citizens comes via contracts with private clinics and hospitals. More and more local authorities are contracting with private firms for their garbage collection. Ambulance service is widely provided as an adjunct of funeral homes. Some communities contract for firefighting, and for management of the city-owned bus company or the airport. Complaints about matters large or small involving public service are likely to come up against a contractual relationship that allows a private firm to determine what benefits the public will receive.

A pessimist would point to the margins of the state as governmental disasters in the making. Yet the picture is not that clear. It is *not* certain that expanding activities on the margins of the state is better or worse than expanding activities in the core departments of the state. The disaster is more clearly in political science than in politics. Professional observers of the state have remained preoccupied with classic issues of elections, legislatures, and executives, when much of the action is elsewhere. There is a prima facie case that bodies on the margins of the state present the greater problems of incoherence. The number of special authorities, government companies, and contractors, each with implicit or explicit grants of autonomy, suggests a high probability of varied procedures and befuddled clients. To go beyond this prima facie case will require political scientists to show the same care in studying the margins that they now devote to research about the core of the state.

Units on the margins of the state have no monopoly on confused control and obscure procedures. If the root problem at the margins is an incoherence of structure that confuses policy makers and clients, there is also plenty of incoherence in the core departments of government.

For example, the Internal Revenue Service — a core agency in the U.S. Department of the Treasury — indicates that befuddled government can result from excessive control and tight accountability between an administrative agency and elected representatives. The Tax Code of the United States is a marvel of rules and exceptions sufficiently complex to support an army of officials in government plus agents in the private sector who concern themselves with the letter and practice of tax policy. Each spring the Internal Revenue Service trumpets its confidence in the compliance of American taxpayers, but shies away from estimating publicly the amount of income that is unreported and untaxed. A variety of simple and complex tax exemptions leads citizens to lawyers, accountants, and storefront tax advisers. These experts are the citizens' contractors, hired to help them get the best deal possible from an incoherent tax code. Some advisers claim only to inform taxpayers about their entitlements according to law and regulations. Others seek to discern the administrative procedures of the Internal Revenue Service. The goal is to learn which items on a return will trigger an audit, and which can slip unexamined through the IRS procedures. These advisers purvey advice on what the taxpayer can get away with in terms of unreported income or inflated reports of expenses. Although such advice is tempting to taxpayers — many of whom chafe at the suspicion that someone else is getting a better deal from the formal rules — it is threatening to the IRS. To protect itself, the IRS adds another bit of sophistication to its audit procedures. It identifies for audit those taxpayers who employ advisers previously identified with many faulty returns. The result looks something like the Egyptian pyramids. Increasingly complex administrative procedures and techniques of avoidance stand as costly public works that offer no tangible benefits to the population.[7]

The Proliferation of Joint Ventures

One feature of modern governments is the partnership between different official bodies. Units can bring different skills and interests to bear on a project, as when health and education specialists deal together on the training of health professionals, or when police and educational units deal with crime in the schools. If two agencies of the government team up to operate a program, the coordination between them might be arranged by their common superiors. With extensive growth on the margins of the state, however, the partners in a joint venture are likely to be lacking a common chain of command that could deal with a problem arising between them.

In Israel, 120 companies are owned by local government authorities, usually in partnership with the national government. (These are a group apart from the 105 companies owned by the national government.) Because local authorities are directly responsible to Jerusalem, there should be lines of supervision upward from municipally owned companies to one or another national ministry. When a senior official of the Interior Ministry—local government supervision is one of its missions—was asked about these companies, he said the Finance Ministry was responsible. Some time later, an equally senior official in the Finance Ministry indicated that the Interior Ministry was responsible. The 1974 report of Israel's State Comptroller singled out these municipal companies for special attention. It noted several lapses in keeping to their own procedures for decision making and financial recordkeeping.

Federal systems such as the United States and Australia have a problem of coordination. The national government and the states are loath to meddle in one another's affairs because of the constitutional gulf between them. Each likes to maintain an image of autonomy. Yet with the proliferation of national programs of aid to the states, coordination becomes a pressing issue. Moreover, many programs of national aid to the states involve units on the margins of one or the other government. State governments in the United States hire contractors to operate federally aided programs because the states do not want to hire permanent civil servants for programs that may be phased out by Washington. With the involvement of two governments plus some bodies on the margins of the state, there is ample opportunity for arrogance and buck-passing in place of coordination.

The General Accounting Office is an agent of the U.S. Congress with wide powers to investigate programs supported by federal monies. High-level officials in the GAO concede, however, that they monitor the activities of national departments and agencies more closely than they do the activities of state governments supported by federal funds. On the state government side, there is often a similar lack of concern about intergovernmental programs. Key budget officials in Wisconsin report that they look closest at programs supported by state tax revenue. Part of the explanation is legitimacy. The officials of each authority express a sense of unease about looking closely at programs that belong partly to someone else. Part of the explanation is each official's efforts to conserve limited resources. Few government bodies have enough time or personnel to take all their responsibilities seriously. When supervisory bodies encounter a joint venture, it is tempting to assume that the other partner will do the supervising. Each conserves its limited resources to look closely at those activities supported entirely by its own money.

In 1977 the newspapers of Melbourne featured an Australian version of this problem with joint ventures: a land scandal at the Victoria

Housing Commission. The problem would have been familiar to any American who had lived on the fringes of Chicago or Boston during the the years of expanding public works. Officials at the Victoria Housing Commission informed their friends of the commission's interest in certain parcels of land. These persons bought the land cheap and then sold dear when the commission publicly announced its intentions. The commission is a statutory authority on the margins of the state government, operating partly through Commonwealth grants. When an official of the state government with nominal responsibility over the commission's activities was asked about the scandal, his first response was, "That's federal money."

The Power of Informal Leaders

With numerous activities spread across the core departments and margins of the modern state, the official leadership may prove unable to control all of them. Indeed, the growth of marginal programs with presumptions of autonomy reflects the growth of government beyond the grasp of the formal governors. These conditions produce informal leadership. Ambition and talent take the place of formal position. Chicago's late Mayor Richard Daley was more than a mayor. His grasp over the use of power went beyond the boundaries of Chicago. He employed some traditional skills of a ward boss plus the vision of a modern grantsman to bring together the various interests of national, state, and local governments to assemble the resources and authority needed for major public works and services.[8]

Richard Daley's power rested on the occupancy of a major elective office. In New York, Robert Moses acquired great power without elective office. His power rested on being appointed to various boards, commissions, and authorities, most of them autonomous and on the margins of state or city government. Robert Moses had great vision for parks, public beaches, highways, and bridges, although he seems to have been blind to the benefits of public transportation and—according to his major biographer—had trouble seeing the needs of blacks and Puerto Ricans.[9] Moses had a genius for working the divided and convoluted city and state units in New York. What to others was ungovernable was to Moses an opportunity. He used his controlling position in certain programs to wheedle even more authority out of politicians, including some—Mayor Fiorello LaGuardia and then-Governor Franklin D. Roosevelt come to mind—who distrusted and possibly detested Moses. Moses was a master at making offers that could not be refused. He persuaded private landowners to donate choice property for his projects, out of the donor's concern that if the land was not donated, the project might be forced through the heart of even more choice holdings. Moses used his knowledge of statutes and his talent as a legislative draftsman to wall off his authorities against interference from elected officeholders. He built toll bridges that brought in far more revenue than needed to pay off bondholders or provide maintenance, and he used the surplus to build more profit-making structures and create a stable of loyal administrators, engineers, and publicists.

Pinhas Sapir exercised his genius astride various bodies of international Jewry and the government of Israel. Sapir headed the Labor Ministry and then the Finance Ministry, but he is best remembered for his little notebook. This book recorded ideas, resources, and opportunities. It listed potential donors and investors from Israel and throughout the world, and the persons or organizations that could use the money. Sapir arranged factories for development towns and eased the transfer of capital across national borders. If the hostility of the country of origin prevented the capital from moving directly to Israel, it made a stop along the way. His personal contacts began to accumulate through his membership in Zionist youth groups in Eastern Europe. They grew via his travels in postwar Western Europe and the Americas. They bore fruit because he was a key figure in the Labor party at a time when it controlled the State of Israel, the Labor Federation, and the World Zionist Organization. Sapir could provide the capital for a government company or a joint venture by the government and the Labor Federation or the Jewish Agency. The Jewish Agency is the body in Israel that receives many of the donations from Jews throughout the world. Occasionally Sapir asked a government company to undertake a venture in order to help out a party colleague, to combat stagnation in a down-at-the-heels agricultural settlement, or to help out a prominent businessman in the diaspora. As long as Sapir had lines to so many sources of capital and so many opportunities for investment, his notebook was each participant's hedge against loss.

WHAT IS THE STATE?

For political scientists, growth on the margins of the state raises an ancient query: *What is the state?* The question is important not only for niceties of theory but for tangible issues of public policy and political influence. How far can the government go in losing control of its own activities without becoming the captive of private firms and individuals? As the head of special authorities, Robert Moses made some decisions with all the independence and arrogance of a nineteenth-century robber baron. Private firms control such "public" services as trash collection, food delivery in government cafeterias, welfare clinics, counseling, and the supervision of criminals on parole. The statutory authorities of Australia and the government-owned companies of Israel provide much of the energy and arteries of transportation that are the sinews of national economies. Occasional breakdowns in these systems have serious consequences for all industries and households. Principles of managerial autonomy have allowed units on the margins to lead their states into serious problems without involving key government leaders. When the voters of a modern state go to the polls, they choose officers who control only a part of the activities done in the name of the state.

Other research, from other branches of political science, also questions the importance of traditional institutions. Such factors as the existence of democracy or authoritarianism do not seem to shape the character of social programs from one country to another. Within the United States, it does not make a great deal of difference for social programs whether a state has competitive political parties or a single dominant party, or whether there is a high or a low level of citizen involvement in elections. Some practitioners in this academic work have asked, "Does politics make a difference?" and have answered in the negative.[10]

The question about the significance of politics is not settled by a long shot. What is clear is that the form of government or the nature of politics is not so powerful an influence on public services that it blots out competing influences from the nature of the economy and the culture of the population.

Some years ago, Fred Riggs came up with the notion of "formalism" to designate the governmental bodies of underdeveloped countries.[11] To Riggs, the elections, legislatures, and prime ministers of Asia, Africa, and Latin America were patterned after forms observed in Europe and North America, but the Third World varieties did not perform like the originals. Often they masked dictatorship or corruption behind the facades of Western democracies. Now we must examine Western democracies in the light of formalism. How many of their public activities are under the control of elections and representative government?

Is this the withering away of the state envisioned by Marxists? There has been a resurgence of radicalism among political scientists who focus on the breakdown-in-process of liberal democratic government. They view the welfare state as a sham, offering workers ameliorations in place of fundamental changes in the structures of government. Adding to the image of collapse are social programs that do not cure poverty, crime rates that continue to rise despite massive police expenditure, and middle-class tax revolts against school bond issues in Ohio or local government in California.[12]

The radical analysis is suggestive, but parts of it are at odds with the problems described here. Control by political elites over enterprises on the margins of the state seem as problematical in the "socialist" East as the "capitalist" West. An equal distribution of incomes, which may be as much of an accomplishment in Israel and Australia as in the Soviet Union, does not save any of those countries from uncontrolled bodies on the margins of their states. In the incoherence of both Eastern and Western welfare states, it is difficult to find evidence of a hidden hand that tilts the flow of goodies from one social class to another. There may be special benefits for those who can learn the system. The bright and well-educated may do well in the face of incoherence. In like manner, wealthy individuals or business firms can hire specialists to help them maximize benefits from complex procedures. Yet corporate giants and their shareholders also encounter problems from the incoherent state. Among the most vexing are shifting judgments with respect to product liability in consumer industries, employer liability for workers' health long after exposure to what had been viewed as safe procedures, and escalating environmental safeguards imposed on industrial plants.

The crisis of political science appears in the failure of the profession to recognize and respond to the growth of bodies on the margins of the state. This is not surprising. Most professions respond slowly, if at all, to fundamental changes in their fields.[13] In fact, there has been considerable awareness of events in the margins. Numerous books and articles describe government-owned companies, special authorities and government contractors.[14] Often the authors recognize the gap in accountability that separates these bodies from the larger political process. What is apparently lacking from the existing literature is the recognition that seemingly different bodies in various countries have traits in common that pose a threat for the state as it is conventionally conceived.

What are the tasks of political scientists in the face of this challenge? First, to codify what is occurring on the margins of the state. At this point, there are only the vaguest of estimates about the size of activities—in terms of expense and work force—on the margins of the state. Second, to identify various patterns with respect to the supervision and control over the margins. At present, there are only scattered reports, most usually indicating dire problems. Those political scientists who are interested in the margins of the state are a long way from being able to compare governance on the margins with that in the core departments of the state. To move beyond prima facie argument supported with illustrations it will be necessary to design studies in a systematic fashion in order to compare units on the margins with those in the core departments of government. It is possible that programs administered on the margins of the state work as well, or better, than those administered by the core departments. On the whole, autonomous managers may respond to a full range of interests better than civil servants who are fully wrapped in red tape. At present we can deal with these issues with little more than feeling and illustration. A sophisticated political scientist must do better.

THE EXTREME CASE OF ISRAEL

Israel is an especially fuzzy case study because of the rich development of its margins. Since its origin in 1948, the State of Israel has been troubled not only by unclear *geographical* boundaries but also by unclear *conceptual* boundaries. Defining the government of Israel is no easy task. Several bodies that are *public* but nongovernmental perform tasks of great importance. There is no clear line between the roles played by certain departments of the state and bodies based in Jewish communities outside Israel. To be sure, no modern state is an island that can be distinguished with absolute clarity from nonstate bodies. Yet Israel's case is extreme. It serves well to illustrate conditions that are not as clear elsewhere.

A major factor in the margin of the Israeli state is the Histadrut, or Labor Federation. Before the government was created, the Labor Federation built systems of public education and medical care, constructed industrial concerns to provide work for its members and new immigrants, established the Workers' Bank to finance other projects, began pension funds, and established cooperatives in agriculture and transportation. The Workers' Bank is now the second largest bank in the country. The Labor Federation's Koor Industries is the largest industrial conglomerate in Israel. The Labor Federation has a role in the two main bus cooperatives and virtually all the country's agriculture. Its companies are partners in joint ventures with numerous government-owned companies. After 1948, the Labor Federation's system of elementary and primary schools was merged with those of the new government, but it has resisted other encroachments by the government. A struggle continues to rage over the "nationalization" of health care. The Labor Federation's Sick Fund enrolls some 75 percent of the population and is a major link between the federation and its membership. The Sick Fund depends heavily on government subsidies established during the long years when the Labor party controlled both the Labor Federation and the Knesset (parliament). Integral to the operation of the Sick Fund are bloated cadres of inefficient clerks and convoluted procedures in the provision of services. But clerks mean jobs, and the Labor Federation remains committed to full employment even at the cost of some efficiency.

The Labor Federation has a full range of political and governmental institutions that parallel those of the government: parliament, executive, controller, and judicial tribunals. It is industrial manager and policy maker as well as spokesman for the workers. It has internal controls to separate functions of company manager and labor representative. But the frequency of wildcat strikes led by rebellious workers' committees suggests the internal problems of the Labor Federation. The many components of the Labor Federation are as unwieldy for its governing council as they are for the government. Much of what stands for public policy making in Israel comes as a result of explicit negotiations or implicit accommodations between officials of the government having formal powers and officials of the Labor Federation having political and economic influence.

Another boundary problem for Israel originates in the Jewish communities of other countries. As the culmination of two thousand years of dreams, prayer, hard politicking, and some fighting, Israel cannot turn its back on the diaspora. A majority of the world's Jews continue to live outside of Israel. Relations between diaspora communities and Israel have ranged from cooperative to contentious. Jewish communities support countless organizations, a few umbrella groups, and many articulate, unfettered individuals. Some diaspora groups and individuals would like to manage the Israeli social and economic programs they support with their contributions. An occasional donor or a leader of a Jewish organization wants to shape Israeli foreign policy. Prominent individuals have urged flexibility or determination on Israel at critical points in her negotiations with Arab neighbors or the United States.

The Jewish Agency is a remnant of the British Mandate in the Middle East. It serves as the Israeli recipient of funds collected overseas by the United Jewish Appeal or United Israel Appeals. The Jewish Agency is structurally distinct from the government of Israel. Like the Labor Federation, however, it controls significant resources. Agency companies participate in several sectors of the economy, and it plays an important role in the provision of social services. The Jewish Agency is responsible to the World Zionist Organization, which is an elected body answerable to constituencies in Israel and the diaspora. Although administrators of the Jewish Agency are mostly resident in Israel, they depend on outsiders, as well as on Israelis, for their mandates. The Jewish Agency is not simply a support. As a result of resolutions passed at the 1978 World Congress of the World Zionist Organization, for example, the Jewish Agency may press for changes in government policy toward orthodox and liberal wings of Judaism. Lest outsiders think this is small stuff for a modern welfare state, they should recall that the government of Prime Minister Yitzhak Rabin fell in 1977 because of a military ceremony that was held too close to the onset of the Sabbath.

A WORD ON ADVANTAGES

The proliferation of government companies, special authorities, and contractors on the margins of the state is not entirely a bad thing. The sheer variety of possible institutions expands the options of policy makers. They can create laws, hire personnel, and design procedures for newly perceived problems without reference to the inclinations of established departments. The chapters in this book on Australia, Israel, and the United States detail numerous benefits that accrue from bodies on the margins of states. Variety also expands the choices available to consumers of public services. This is a good thing for individuals and business firms that are able to perceive and select from the full menu of what is offered.[15] For others, however, diversity may only be confusing, or may cause bitterness when it is seen that someone else gets a better deal. The incoherent welfare state may produce an inequality based on the knowledge of complex procedures and the skills needed to work the system.

PROSPECTS FOR REFORM

There is no end to reform schemes aimed at improving the operation of welfare states. Many of these suggestions would alleviate problems. Many others would add to overall complexity without solving the problems they tackle.

The ombudsman is both a reflection on and a partial remedy for the incoherent state. The job of an ombudsman is to help individuals receive proper service from complex institutions.[16] The ombudsman should help a citizen who feels he has not been treated fairly. The ombudsman seeks to clarify the citizen's case and brings pressure against an errant bureaucrat. Yet the ombudsman comes into a case only *after* a citizen feels wronged. An ombudsman cannot tell a confused citizen where to obtain service from a maze of agencies with confusing titles. Furthermore, the ombudsman, too, may be frustrated by incoherence. The 1976 report of Israel's national ombudsman comments about local offices that had failed to enforce proper decisions in spite of court orders and repeated contacts by the ombudsman. Israelis may also face confusion because of the multiplicity of ombudsmen. In Israel there is a national ombudsman located in the office of the State Comptroller plus specialized ombudsmen in certain ministries plus municipal ombudsmen in larger cities. Citizens who seek redress need a certain amount of knowledge and determination to work through the agencies established to help them.

Many people face problems before it is appropriate to call in an ombudsman. With a variety of government departments and institutions on the margins of the state, people do not know where to begin in asking for service. To help them, a number of American communities have set up multiple agency referral centers. Here a client can drop in, describe his problems, and hope for directions to the proper office. Of course, the client must first know about the existence of the multiple referral center. Australians have set up similar units, and their terminology may increase visibility. Australians advertise their referral agencies as "One-Stop Shops."

Australians may be clever about helping citizens find their way through the service maze, but they have also created problems for government officials charged with overseeing the margins of their state. Parliaments of both Commonwealth and state governments have created unique statutes to control the activities of many special authorities. A continuing process of amendment allows new issues to be defined by law. The legislation passes the democratic test of being public and reviewable by lawmakers and citizens. Yet the diversity of conditions established for each authority hinders the work of government officials. The people who really understand each statute are the ranking officials, the very people who are supposedly being regulated. At times they bluff their way through encounters with political superiors, claiming to be operating under mandates that are not clearly stated in the statute. A politician or senior government official will think twice before challenging an authority's manager over an issue of statutory interpretation. The time spent mastering a railway statute could prohibit any other work. And if the next encounter is with an electricity authority, the official must begin again with another complex statute. Americans have their own experiences with reforms that promise improvements for citizens or officials, but in reality only change the shape of serious problems. Advisers to President Franklin Roosevelt perceived that the President needed more staff assistance to help him manage the sprawling federal bureaucracy. They began a process that culminated in the Imperial Presidencies of Lyndon Johnson and Richard Nixon. Executive staffs grew beyond the tolerance of cabinet secretaries, members of Congress, and perhaps the President himself. No one can be sure whether one of the hundreds of assistants accustomed to speaking in the name of the White House is actually carrying the authority of the President or working a deal for someone else. Congress, too, has its problems with bloated staffs hired to cope with an awesome executive branch. Recent figures record 18,300 individuals on the payrolls of the House and Senate.

The future of incoherence seems likely to be one of continuous tinkering and more complexity. If the motive forces of incoherence are the demands of citizens for services and the commitments of elected officials to respond positively, then we are in for more agencies of government and even more units put on the margins of the state by policy makers who feel they must surrender some of their opportunities to supervise and control.

The work of tinkerers bears some likeness to the Australians' experiences with rabbits and blackberries. Both were imported to Australia in the nineteenth century in order to enrich the diets of settlers. Both multiplied far beyond the settlers' capacities to use or control them, and both came to be outlawed as agricultural pests.

Another story from Australia suggests the inevitability of suffering the consequences of the welfare state even as we appreciate its advantages and add to its offerings. During a downpour in Melbourne someone was heard to ask, "Do you know what they do in Sydney when it rains like this?"

The answer was, "They get wet!"

THIS BOOK

While bloated margins and general incoherence seem to be universal problems of modern states, they also differ greatly in detail from place to place. The next three chapters deal with growth on the margins of the state in Australia, Israel, and the United States. The choice of these countries owes much to the good fortune of research opportunity. Yet each country makes heavy use of certain kinds of institutions built on the margins of the state in order to provide many of the services demanded by citizens. Each format is widely used throughout the modern world. Therefore the patterns found in Australia, Israel, and the United States represent a slice of experience larger than their own.

The chapter on Australia features the statutory authorities created by Commonwealth and state governments, especially those of the State of Victoria. This is the simplest of the cases presented here, for it has the clearest lines of control from government officials to the margins of the state. This clarity largely reflects the law-abiding political culture of Australia, and the conservative views executives hold about their opportunities for discretion.

The chapter on Israel concentrates on government participation in limited-liability companies, with extensions into subsidiaries and joint ventures between companies of the government, the Labor Federation, the Jewish Agency, and other investors. The traits of the Israeli case come partly from the peculiar experience of that country with multiple "public sectors" and partly from the entrepreneurialism of public officials that finds its roots in Jewish culture.

The chapter on the United States deals both with government contractors and with special authorities. Government contracting with private industry and nonprofit bodies owes something to Americans' antipathy to government. The United States has built an extensive and generous welfare state imbued with free enterprise. Special authorities also owe something to the antigovernment motif of American government, as well as to the autonomy of state and local governments. The American scene is the most incoherent we study; issues of management and political accountability are made especially complex by elected officials who compete openly among themselves and frustrate one another's efforts to control the margins of the state.

Considerable differences can be seen between statutory authorities in Australia, government shareholding in limited-liability companies in Israel, and government contracting plus special authorities in the United States. Academic specialists in each field would prefer three or four books, rather than one. Other differences appear within each type. By concentrating on certain statutory authorities from the State of Victoria, we sacrifice the rich variety that would come from a survey of the five other Australian states and the Commonwealth government. In the chapter on the United States, examples come disproportionately from the experiences of the national government and the state government of Wisconsin. Materials on Israel deal mostly with companies owned by the government and slight many fascinating cases from the other "public sectors": the Labor Federation, and the Jewish Agency. The reader should bear with this rude assemblage of different countries and institutions and recognize their common traits. The focus is on bodies that appear on the margins of the state with formal or actual autonomy from the conventional organs of democratic governance. They add to the general phenomenon of incoherence in modern welfare states, which befuddles officials and citizens and creates problems of management and political accountability.

The target of this book is as much the crisis in political science as the crisis in the modern state. Units on the margins of the state offer great benefits to policy makers and citizens. On balance, they may be more beneficial than problematical. The crisis in political science is more clear. Until we learn more about institutions that are from, but not of, the state, we delude ourselves with a false sense of understanding public policy. We learn less and less of *Who rules?* and *Who gets what?* by continued studies of conventional government or the politics that takes place among elected officials.

2

AUSTRALIA: STATUTORY AUTHORITIES AND LAW-ABIDING MANAGERS

One definition of the good life is "Australia." Australia may be the richest country in the world, and an affluent life style is spread evenly throughout the population. The high standard of living results from a well-educated work force and a land of fabulous natural resources. Australians do not have to work hard in order to be comfortable. The pursuit of leisure competes with personal advancement as the national trait.[1]

Because they are a long way from most modern states, and inward-looking, Australians also avoid the defense burdens that weigh on less fortunate societies. Military expenditures take less than 3 percent of gross domestic product, an amount that is small change compared with the demands of the Israeli Defense Ministry or the U.S. Department of Defense.

The wealth and security of Australia can be seen in its public life. Citizens receive services of high quality. Government-owned transportation is clean and usually on time. Support for higher education and the arts is generous by international standards. Public radio and television are excellent. Health insurance is universal and extensive in its coverage of hospital and clinic treatments. Government departments and statutory authorities provide roomy and attractive areas in which to receive the public, and occasionally enrich the architectural scene with new construction. Working conditions are good throughout the public services, and approach the opulent at the upper reaches. Public service salaries compare favorably with those in other well-to-do countries, and approximate incomes at the upper reaches of the private sector. High marginal tax rates at upper-income levels and cost-of-living adjustments every three or six months work to maintain equality and purchasing power throughout the society. Senior academics, civil servants, and business executives do not have the spread in salary seen in their counterparts in the United States; there is even less of a salary spread after the Australians have paid taxes at rates of 62.9 percent on taxable incomes above $32,000.[2]

In Australia the atmosphere in government offices and statutory authorities is one of genteel respect for professional norms and orderly procedure. There is little overt sign of upward striving on the part of executives, and little mobility from one organization to another. This is partly the result of a culture that restricts serious competition to the squash court or golf course, but it also reflects pension schemes that impose severe penalties on mid-career changes in employment. There may be little financial reward and considerable loss in retirement benefits to be had from changing jobs. It is also difficult to jump over the seniority queue that governs most promotions. A high-flyer might break into an organization at the upper levels, but he will do so at the cost of some hostility from his new colleagues, which might weigh against future advancement.

Australian officials do not cut corners in pursuing achievements for themselves or their organizations. They express a narrow view of what is permitted to them. When asked about the meaning of law, they say they can do only what is explicitly authorized in the statutes. More aggressive views — for example, that an organization can do anything not explicitly prohibited by the law, or that a manager should make decisions and then seek a way to implement them through the legal niceties — are seldom heard.

In sum, Australia's public servants show few signs of entrepreneurship. That it is lacking can be seen from their behavior, their views toward law, and their sense of humor. One senior management group made no response to the following story about entrepreneurialism included in a luncheon talk on administrative cultures. The story concerned British and American shoe salesmen sent by their firms to a new

Third World nation. The Britisher cabled to his home office soon after arriving: *Natives wear no shoes. Am returning on next ship.* The American was equally quick in cabling to his home office: *Natives wear no shoes. Send 300 dozen pair.* This story has evoked a lively response from Israeli and American audiences; it produced only silence from the Australians.

Curiosities and anomalies exist in the public life of Australia. In spite of the paucity of objective conditions for class-based political dispute there is lively ideological debate and chronic labor unrest. Recent years have seen interruptions of mail service, strikes on railways and bus lines, and airport closings resulting from job actions by traffic controllers. In the winter of 1977 a strike by maintenance workers caused a month-long rationing of electricity in Victoria. This cut rail and tram service to half schedule, blacked out most radio and television — with an exception granted for a crucial football match — limited home heating and lighting, and cut all power to industry. Half a million workers (47 percent of Victoria's work force and 13 percent of the national work force) were out of work for four weeks.

It is difficult to reconcile an affluent and egalitarian society with a high level of dispute. Much of the conflict traces to imported ideologies having little fit in the Australian setting. Several unions have communist leaders. There is an active anti-freeway lobby against American-style roads that seem out of keeping with the archaic and congested road system of Australia. Environmentalists are as feisty in the clean air of Australian cities as they are in Los Angeles. The State Electricity Commission of Victoria has seen its work on an inner-city generating plant slowed to a crawl by labor union bans since 1974, in spite of having received all the permits required by environmental legislation. One noisy issue is a campaign to stop the mining and export of uranium; arguments focus on the implications of Australian uranium for the ecology and weaponry of Europe and Asia. Campaigners have won the support of dockworkers and blocked shipments from Melbourne and Sydney.

More ideological sound and fury than real threat is evident in Australian public life. There is the inconvenience of frequent strikes and poor roads, but little danger of great change in the economy or society. While the noise is great, the Labour party is weak. At the Commonwealth level, it has held power in only three of the past twenty-seven years. Labour currently enjoys majorities in the lower houses of two state Parliaments but does not have a majority in any upper house.

THE LAND, THE PEOPLE, AND THE GOVERNMENT

The continent-country of Australia is about the size and shape of the United States (excluding Alaska). Australia is marked not only by great natural wealth but also by geographical isolation. It is a long way from potential adversaries — even longer when distances are estimated from the heavily populated areas along the southeastern coast. Sydney is more than 3400 miles from Jakarta, 4900 miles from Tokyo, 5400 miles from Peking, and 5700 miles from Calcutta. Europe is clear on the other side of the world and North America almost as far.

In aggregate terms, the population of Australia is sparse. Some 14 million people inhabit almost 3 million square miles, which produces a statistical average of 5 persons to every square mile. Yet few people live in the vast, desertlike interior. Eight and one half million live in the capital cities of the six states, which makes Australia one of the most urbanized nations on earth. All told, 58 percent of the population lives in cities of at least 500,000 population. Each state has one major metropolitan center, with most of the people living over hundreds of suburban square miles in single family homes surrounded by small gardens.

Great Britain and Ireland have provided the bulk of Australia's population, particularly of those settlers who arrived before World War II. Since then, large numbers have come from southern Europe; Italy, Greece, Yugoslavia, and Turkey are prominent in the new migrations. Depending on economic circumstances, Australia is more or less hospitable to immigrants. When labor is scarce, the gates open and the government may even subsidize the passage of prospective migrants. When jobs become scarce, the government grants visas with a sharp eye for the skills needed.

The Commonwealth of Australia dates back only to 1901. Earlier there were six colonies of Great Britain, two of whose histories of European settlement go back to 1787 and 1803 (New South Wales and Tasmania). Before becoming a nation, the colonies had separate and colorful histories. The transportation of convicts figured prominently in New South Wales and Tasmania; South Australia is proud of its early experiments in community planning; Queensland experienced a large-scale importation of labor from South Pacific islands to tropical plantations along its north coast; Victoria had a gold rush and folk-hero bandits not unlike the wild days of the American West; and in Western Australia the isolation that marks all of Australia to some degree has persisted in exaggerated form. Western Australia's capital, Perth, is over 1300 miles from the nearest large city (Adelaide in South Australia).

Federation was a natural form of government for Australia. There were great distances between the population centers of each state plus many decades of separate development. Even the railroads of each state were built to different gauges, which still complicates transportation from one part of the Commonwealth to another.

To an American visitor, Australia's federation is somewhat familiar, for the government is modeled partly after the United States and partly after Great Britain. British roots appear in the parliamentary form of government at both national (Commonwealth) and state levels. The Commonwealth head of state is the Governor General and that of the state is the Governor. Both are appointed by the British monarch on the advice of the national or state governments. The roles of these heads of state are more often symbolic than tangible, but they do hold residual powers with respect to the appointment and dismissal of the working governments. Governments at both national and state levels are created out of the leading parties in the Parliaments. The Prime Minister heads the Commonwealth government; his state government counterpart is the Premier.

American roots can be seen in the federation, which has a written constitution that assigns to each level of government its major roles. Unlike the United States, Australian federalism has not developed strong notions of local autonomy. The state governments of Australia have principal charge of services like police, education, and land-use planning, which are governed locally in most of the United States.

Victoria provides the setting for most of the statutory authorities considered in this chapter. Smallest of the mainland states, Victoria is at the extreme southeast corner of the continent, just north of the island state of Tasmania. Melbourne is the capital of Victoria and its dominant city. Together with its suburbs, Melbourne accounts for 73 percent of the state's population of 3.7 million. Manufacturing, commerce, and finance are prominent in Melbourne's economy. Victoria is the most uniformly watered of the mainland states; both grains and livestock are important features of the rural sector. Victoria has not experienced the booming mineral finds that have put other parts of Australia at the center of world mineral exploration in recent years. Nevertheless, its nineteenth-century history featured a spectacular gold rush, and the state has extensive deposits of brown coal and natural gas.

THE MARGINS OF THE
AUSTRALIAN STATE

The margins of the Australian state are heavily populated with statutory authorities. A committee of the Australian Senate could find no comprehensive list of organizations required to report to Parliament; it also found some that did not submit annual reports.[3] The committee did identify 220 institutions, but only after combing through law books, annual reports, government publications, and the telephone books. Employees of the statutory authorities totaled over 220,000, compared with some 155,000 employees of Commonwealth ministries and departments.[4] In Victoria the margins are also larger than core units of the state government. More than 80 statutory authorities employ about 102,000 people, against 25 ministries and departments with 19,500 employees in the state government. Victoria claims to be the home of the statutory authority, for Victorian Railways was organized in 1856.[5] From there the device spread to other Australian colonies, to the United Kingdom, and elsewhere. Almost all of Australia's public enterprises are organized as statutory authorities. An exception is Qantas Airlines, a limited-liability company with a majority of shares held by the Commonwealth. This oddity traces to circumstances in the history of Qantas, but is made less significant as formal agreements between the airline's management and the Commonwealth Treasury take the place of the statutes that govern other authorities.

The statutory authorities of Australia are also called "instrumentalities," although "statutory authority" is the more distinctive and more widely used term. These authorities are created by acts of the Commonwealth or by state Parliaments, and are set apart from the ministries and departments at the core of Commonwealth and state governments. Details of each authority's control by government are set down in statutes that differ considerably from one authority to another. In the words of the *Yearbook* published by the State of Victoria:

The general features of the instrumentalities are constitutions by Act of Parliament, a controlling Board or Commission appointed by the Governor in Council, freedom from direct ministerial control over day to day administration (but subject to governmental or ministerial control in matters of major policy, and subject in some cases to the approval of the Governor in Council or the Minister), and control over the appointment of staff and the de-

termination of salaries and other conditions of employment. Financial arrangements differ considerably.[6]

With careful attention to the punctuation and qualifications in this official description, a reader may become sensitive to the great variety of form and practice to be found in the statutory authorities of Victoria and other jurisdictions of Australia. The official description notes that acts of Parliament define certain features of each authority. Yet the authorities are free in matters of day-to-day administration, the appointment of staff, the determination of salaries and other working conditions. The differences in law and practice that define each authority result in a great variety of financial arrangements. Some authorities support themselves on revenues from their operations; others depend on government subsidies. Some have independent bank accounts; others depend on government officials to keep their books and issue checks.

A resident of Melbourne encounters statutory authorities at every turn. As indicated in table 1, authorities of the Commonwealth or state governments provide mass transportation, road construction, water, sewage, and town planning; finance hospital construction; broadcast on radio and television; build housing; offer a wide range of banking services; and generate and distribute electricity and household gas.

Table 1

Major Statutory Authorities in the Melbourne Area, By Field of Service and Government Responsible

ENERGY
> State Electricity Commission (*State of Victoria*)
> Gas and Fuel Corporation (*State of Victoria*)

TRANSPORT
> Melbourne and Metropolitan Tramways Board (*State of Victoria*)
> County Roads Board (*State of Victoria*)
> Victorian Railways (*State of Victoria*)
> Qantas Airlines (*Commonwealth of Australia*)
> Trans-Australia Airlines (*Commonwealth of Australia*)

COMMUNICATION
Australian Telecommunications Commission (*Commonwealth of Australia*)
Australian Postal Commission (*Commonwealth of Australia*)
Australian Broadcasting Commission (*Commonwealth of Australia*)

HEALTH AND SANITATION
Hospitals and Charities Commission (*State of Victoria*)
Melbourne and Metropolitan Board of Works (*State of Victoria*)

HOUSING AND LAND DEVELOPMENT
Housing Commission (*State of Victoria*)
Melbourne and Metropolitan Board of Works (*State of Victoria*)
Victoria State Bank (*State of Victoria*)

PLANNING
Melbourne and Metropolitan Board of Works (*State of Victoria*)

ECONOMIC DEVELOPMENT
Virtually all of the above plus
Commonwealth Banking Corporation (*Commonwealth of Australia*)

EDUCATION
Various universities and colleges of advanced education (*State of Victoria*)

Statutory authorities play important roles in virtually every sector of the economy except retailing and manufacturing. In the development of Australia, the government has assumed a dominant position in the operation of infrastructure and the exploitation of mineral and energy resources. Only minor units of the Commonwealth government manufacture defense material or related products. The Government Aircraft Factory pursues several lines of civilian production in order to preserve its skills as a national resource in the event of war. The remainder of light and heavy manufacturing and retailing is in the private sector, with much of it owned by American, British, or Japanese multinationals. The government plays an active role in protecting local manufacture through high tariffs. It protects retailing by enforcing shopping hours. Virtually everything but the corner grocer must close most weekday evenings, Saturday afternoon, and all day Sunday.

All major political parties have endorsed and expanded the government's role via statutory authorities. The Liberal party purveys free enterprise rhetoric, but makes exceptions for the kinds of government intervention that are traditionally Australian.[7] Victoria is the most consistently Liberal-dominated state in the country, but it has as extensive a collection of statutory authorities as any other jurisdiction.

Statutory authorities dominate visibly. The architecture of downtown Melbourne features the imposing Victorian facade of the Victorian Railway headquarters plus the striking glass and stone of the State Electricity Commission and the Melbourne and Metropolitan Board of Works. Affluence appears inside as well as on the outside of statutory authorities. Executive suites, which are large, richly paneled, and thickly carpeted, have well-stocked liquor cabinets and dining rooms. Some authorities maintain extensive rural properties with farms and lodges used for the entertainment of visitors and ranking managers. A high-level official of an authority is likely to have a car among his perquisites, and those at the very top will have a chauffeur as well.

Statutory authorities also figure among the prominent topics of public controversy. In 1960 a University of Melbourne political scientist wrote about the statutory authorities that "their policies, and not the departments', make up the fast-moving current in Victorian politics."[8] In 1978, another political scientist from the university reported on formal inquiries into four of the state's statutory authorities. Based on the previous six months, the inquiries dealt with the costly strike at the State Electricity Commission, a land scandal in the Housing Commission, proposals to reconstitute the Melbourne and Metropolitan Board of Works, and physical deterioration in a highway project of the Country Roads Board.[9]

The liveliest political scandal for newspaper readers in Melbourne has concerned the land dealings of the State Housing Commission. One consortium of developers sold a block of land to the commission for $3.4 million, after buying it three weeks earlier for $1.8 million. Another consortium, which included a former aide to a state government minister, sold land to the commission for $4.6 million that it had bought over the previous eighteen months for $1.8 million. Much of this land was prone to flooding and not suited to residential construction. There were also payments and gifts from land developers to commission employees. The scandal erupted on this clean and upright political system like an ill wind from its sordid past. Land booming was common among developers and officials in the last decades of the nineteenth century, with greatly inflated prices and overbuilding of suburban railroads and other public facilities preceding sudden collapses in prices and fortunes.[10] The official report into the 1977 scandal was circumspect in its treatment of responsible ministers, although it recommended criminal proceedings be taken against some commission employees.[11]

One of the more extraordinary political figures in Victoria today is Alan Croxford, chairman of the Melbourne and Metropolitan Board of Works since 1966. Stories about him that circulate among area journalists, politicians, academics, and civil servants include

Allegations of land deals that bring great profit to Croxford, members of his family, and close associates

Personal use of the Board of Works farm and holiday lodge

Sharp and deceptive dealing in assembling coalitions to support controversial projects among members of his governing board

Meddling in technical details that should be left to board employees

Behind some of these allegations are of course the hurt feelings of politicians left out of coalitions Croxford has put together. Behind others may be simple disagreements over policy. One member of a suburban municipal council expressed intense negative feelings about the aesthetic details of a local park Croxford had designed.

Perhaps most important in explaining Croxford's reputation is the centrality of the Board of Works to critical decisions of metropolitan development. The structure of the board, until recently governed by fifty-four representatives of municipal councils, has encouraged a wheeler-dealer leadership style. Croxford is active in decisions that affect the allocation of large amounts of public funds and projects with immense implications for private profits. Allegations about his behavior prompted two formal inquiries between 1966 and 1977. Croxford emerged whole from both inquiries, and remains chairman of the Board of Works. As a result of the most recent inquiry, the structure of the board was changed. It is now governed by a seven-member body appointed by the state government.

THE AUSTRALIAN ENVIRONMENT
AND THE AUTHORITIES

It seems inevitable that a national setting will influence the kinds of institutions that appear on the margins of a state. The question is: Which traits of the environment are likely to be important?

Some clues come from studies of public policies within the United States. Comparisons from one U.S. state to another suggest that economic traits, the political culture, and the nature of government have something to do with the kinds of policies offered residents.[12] I borrow from these findings in order to organize a comparison of units on the margins of Australia, Israel, and the United States.

Political Culture

Political culture is a useful concept that includes attitudes and behavior with respect to public affairs. Admittedly, culture is a vague concept; analyses of it often suffer from a lack of hard evidence. What at first sight seems to be a country's political culture may be an ambiguous combination of different tendencies. It may be difficult to show that certain traits are part of a general culture and not part of a distinct subculture or an isolated example. Yet, with all its looseness, the use of political culture has wide appeal. Populations differ from one another in their attitude and behavior patterns, often in ways that fit together in cultural patterns.

The political culture of Australia has a British flavor. In spite of the large-scale immigration from southern Europe since World War II, the inflow is being absorbed into British mores. Almost all the surnames encountered in the upper reaches of government and the statutory authorities came from somewhere in the British Isles. Also in the British mode is the Australian's profound respect for written law and conservative view of what law permits. Formality in procedure appears along with formality in dress and styles of communication. There is a touch of elitism. Senior civil servants are conscious of their status and are not inclined to compromise their position with an informality in dress or a too-ready use of first names. A tough libel law helps preserve the decorum of public affairs. The media are reluctant to charge wrongdoing by individual officeholders without substantial evidence in hand. Passivity in the face of opportunity and a concern to protect the status quo are more apparent than entrepreneurship.

Signs of these cultural traits appear in the acceptance of formal agreements as key instruments in defining the scope of activities on the margins of the Australian state. There is a genteel style of restrained conflict that is evident in executive offices and in dealings between the statutory authorities and state and Commonwealth governments. Senior government officials defer to the statutory authorities. If disputes about the relative power of authorities or government offices occur, they do so in private, with losers content to justify the influence of winners. There is also a passive acceptance by personnel of limited career opportunities.

Government: Federation

The aspect of Australian *government* that makes itself felt most clearly on the statutory authorities is federalism. Australia was six separate colonies long before it was a nation, and the symbols and substance of state governments remain strong nearly eighty years after federation. Statutory authorities of the state governments dominate in the energy field and in surface transportation, and are strong in banking. Interstate economic competition prompted the creation of several authorities in order to assure their home states an adequate supply of certain goods or services.[13] State authorities discriminate in favor of home-state suppliers in their bidding contracts. State railroads continue to show the effect of separate design: Queensland's rail gauge is 3 feet 6 inches, that of New South Wales is 4 feet 8.5 inches, and Victoria's is 5 feet 3 inches. Although an interstate standard-gauge line runs from Brisbane south and west to Perth, much traffic halts at state boundaries while crews shift carriages from one gauge to another.

The federal nature of Australia's government has much to do with financial controls that bear on the statutory authorities of state governments. Such firms encounter Commonwealth as well as state procedures when they seek capital for expansion, which occurs annually for enterprises that deal in electricity, gas supply, water and sewer lines, railways, and housing. The Loan Council is the key body. Made up of the Prime Minister and all state Premiers, the Loan Council monitors the impact of public activities on the national economy.[14] State enterprises compete with one another for shares of their state's borrowing authority. Formal procedures are laid down in the Financial Agreement between the Commonwealth and the States, and in a "gentlemen's agreement" pertaining to borrowing by statutory authorities and local governments. The mechanics are complex, but the code of behavior emphasizes restraint in the assertion of one's position.

Each state's treasury receives demands from its enterprises and government departments for loan authority and submits a consolidated demand to the Commonwealth Treasury. The Commonwealth Treasury then works up a position for the Prime Minister, which is governed by macroeconomic considerations, a desire to keep each state's share of the total more or less constant, and a recognition of the special project needs presented by individual states. The Commonwealth Treasury's powerful role partly reflects the voting structure of the Loan Council. Each state Premier has one vote, and the Commonwealth Prime Minister has two votes plus a casting vote in case of ties. The Prime Minister's role in the Loan Council is bolstered further by the Commonwealth's domination of fiscal policy making and by its monopoly of the personal income tax that supplies grants to state governments.

On their side, state enterprises tend to observe two rules of restraint. First, they make their appeals to state personnel only; they do not jump out of line to approach Canberra directly. Second, they flog their own demands, emphasizing what program targets will not be met and what dire consequences will befall the public if their demands for capital are not accepted by the state and the Loan Council. They stop short of attacking other enterprises' demands as being less important than their own. State and Commonwealth government bodies also do their part to make the contest benign. Commonwealth officials assess the magnitude of each state's requests but refrain from commenting on within-state allocations determined by state personnel. Generally the rules of incrementalism prevail. Each state and each enterprise counts on the same amount of borrowing authority that it had last year plus a percentage increment to be decided in Canberra and by the state's treasury. The Commonwealth agreed in 1978 to liberalize borrowing by state instrumentalities outside Australia.

The federal nature of Australian government is familiar to Americans; the absence of local autonomy is less familiar. Important services provided in local communities come mostly from state government departments or statutory authorities. Police and education are state functions, as is town planning, water supply, and sewage for metropolitan areas. Thus, a body like the Melbourne and Metropolitan Board of Works, a statutory authority of Victoria, is in the midst of community squabbles over planning and land use.

Economy

The *wealth* of Australia lurks behind several features of its statutory authorities. The quality of their physical plants and the smooth running of most services is apparent to anyone who has seen the public enterprises of poor countries. The acceptance by managers of stable career structures, rather than an entrepreneurial pursuit of achievement, may have something to do with the affluence as well as with the passivity of the culture. Australian managers have a good life that includes plenty of time for leisure, enough money for a place in the country, long hours at the beach, and membership in a sports club. Striving for advancement may quicken the pace up the corporate ladder, but at some cost in lost "mateship."

THE NATURE OF AUSTRALIA'S MARGINS

The most prominent feature of units on the margins of the Australian state[15] is their character as statutory authorities. Their statutes are crucial. An act of the Commonwealth or state Parliament defines the purpose of each authority and details its governing structure, the powers of its various officials, the lines of control between the authority and organs of the Commonwealth or state government, and a variety of minutiae as to what the authority may or may not do with respect to its services. The length of the statutes gives a clue to their detailed nature. Almost all important bodies have statutes of at least sixty pages; some go over a hundred pages. Statutes may identify salary grades for individual officers, set the number of positions to be included in each authority's roster, define prices to the public for various services, and authorize specific projects. Among the matters covered in the statute of the State Electricity Commission of Victoria are

The size of the bank overdraft to be allowed the commission

Authority for the commission to sell electrical apparatus or briquette burning apparatus

Authority for the commission to undertake various specified construction projects

Authority for the commission to license electrical mechanics, and the specification of fines for carrying out such work without a license

Provisions for local government around the mining works of the commission

Details of relationships between the State Electricity Commission and other state government entities with which the commission comes in contact

The statute of an authority is its constitution and bylaws, and the principal means of control employed by the Commonwealth or state government. Acts are changed frequently; there can be one or more amendments each year for prominent authorities. Such changes reflect not only the importance of the statute as a means of governmental control but also the disinclination of managers to move far without the authority granted by a specific amendment. The source of amendments is likely to be the managers. They do not always get what they want from the government, but it is usually they who initiate changes. To some extent the origin of amendments begs the question: *Who is in control?* Although many changes are initiated from within the authorities, their concern to formalize changes via statutory amendment indicates their sense of dependence on law. One manager expressed a view of his statute that represents the feeling of many colleagues: "It must be explicitly permitted in the statute, or clearly derivable from the language of the statute. If it's not in the law, we don't do it."

The function of the statute has some component of "covering" actions initiated by a manager, as well as controlling his actions. No one in government is likely to know a statute as well as the top executives of an authority. At times, managers assert that some power lies within their complex statute in order to deter a politician from imposing unwanted instructions. By the time the politician has the opportunity to check the statute, the issue may no longer be timely.

At one cabinet meeting to discuss responses to a strike in a major authority, a minister proposed a curtailment of all the authority's services. He wanted to bring the pressure of public opinion against the strikers. The proposal was heroic, but probably dangerous to those elements of the state's economy and population that might otherwise escape from the strike with little more than inconvenience. In the heat of discussion, the chairman of the involved authority defused the suggestion by asserting that it was contrary to the statute. He maintained that Parliament would have to amend the statute to justify a complete stoppage of service. In fact, the proposal of the cabinet member was not clearly contrary to the authority's statute, but the reputation of the authority's chairman for forthright dealing and intimate knowledge of his business carried the day. What may have been a daring but desperate proposal died after being stunned by statutory language that no one could refute.

The use of statutory controls over institutions on the margins of the state has certain advantages for democratic theory. The statutes are public and open to debate. They allow control in large or small detail, depending on the interest of the government. They facilitate the work of various officials in the Treasury and other departments of government, who must approve authority actions before they occur or monitor authority activities already under way. The statutes specify the substance of authority activities and describe the consultations that must occur between the authority and government officials.

The Diversity of Authorities

The Commonwealth and state governments have produced authorities of great variety. According to one observer, "like flowers in spring... they have grown so variously and profusely and with as little regard for conventional patterns... a new species often suggests a new genus."[16]

Some of the ninety authorities of the Commonwealth government must conduct their finances within the government accounts, whereas others can have their own bank accounts. Some authorities are financed wholly or mainly by the government, whereas others make their own way as business enterprises. Some of those thought of as business enterprises are expected to return a profit to the Commonwealth, whereas others are expected only to break even. Some authorities have no financial directives in their statutes.

One specialist in the statutory authorities of Western Australia notes that "the law of statutory corporations is a wilderness of single instances."[17] The official *Manual of Government Finance in Western Australia* concedes that "there are no rules or principles... it is purely a matter of what appeared at the time to be the most suitable administrative arrangement."[18] As in other states, the statutory authorities of Western Australia vary greatly in the number of people sitting on their boards of directors (from more than twenty to only one), in the procedures used for appointing senior personnel, and in the sources of authority funds.[19] Authorities may read their statutes closely in order to restrict or to defend themselves. Just as they may go no further than allowed in expanding their activities, they may go no further than required in facilitating control by the government. For example, a committee of the Australian Senate cited Qantas and Trans-Australia Airlines for refusing its request for financial information on the narrow claim of the firms that they do not receive government monies of the kinds being investigated.[20]

Problems of Statutory Control

The prominence of the statutes as means of control has contributed to the attenuation of government units that are important in other countries. Neither Israeli nor American governments rely so heavily on explicit legal controls over the margins of their states. Neither do Israeli nor American governments deal with managers who are so law-abiding in their attitudes and behaviors. In both Israel and the United States, central organs are more aggressive than they are in Australia in seeking information from units on the margin, and in adjusting control procedures to meet the realities of noncompliance. Auditors in both Israel and the United States monitor the management and the service delivery of organizations, including those on the margins of the state. They collect details about program effectiveness and efficiency, as well as conventional financial reports. In Australia, Auditors-General of Commonwealth and state governments issue only thin financial reports about their government departments and rely on commercial firms to audit statutory authorities.

One state ombudsman in Australia finds that he can rely on statutory authorities to monitor their own activities. He feel that authorities are responsive to client complaints and generally comply with their statutes. The ombudsman focuses his attention on ministries of the government, and refers complaints about statutory authorities to their own personnel. The ombudsman does not count among his own actions cases handled routinely by statutory authorities. This is of a piece with the deference and lack of assertiveness found elsewhere in Australia. Such arrangements are not adequate for the Israeli national ombudsman. A great deal of his activity focuses on government-owned companies, some of which are among the most popular targets for citizen complaints.

Some Australian officials express unease about their lack of control capacity, although they may express general confidence in the integrity of statutory authorities. One auditor-general admitted that he knew little about the authorities beyond what he read in the reports of commercial audit firms. This is less than he can learn about shareholder-owned companies in the private sector of Australia! His point has gen-

eral application to controls over the units on the margins of his state
and others. Because they are *of* the state, these bodies are not subject
to those requirements of financial disclosure imposed on private corporations for the protection of investors.[21] Because these bodies are
not exactly *in* the state, however, they escape many of the detailed
controls over departmental operations. Their distinction from both
core departments of government and business firms of the private sector bestows on them unique independence. They have much of the freedom enjoyed by the independent corner grocer, even though they
operate with the protection of government monopoly and access to
government capital.

It reflects the passive nature of Australian officials that this same
auditor-general indicated his willingness to wait for a groundswell of
demand for enlarged audit procedures. His counterparts in Israel and the
United States, in contrast, have led the movements in their countries
— and have preached in international forums of state auditors— to
upgrade auditing from a narrow concern for compliance with financial
norms to a broader concern with management and program effectiveness.[22]

The specificity of statutes gets in the way of effective control. Each
authority works under a unique statute, and the vast number of them
makes it impossible for control officers in government to comprehend
all the statutes that fall within their responsibility. One senior official
lamented when he pointed to a bookcase filled with statutes of several
dozen authorities, "I don't know what's in those." For the most part, he
relies on a general sense of what each statute provides. Much of his information about each statute comes from executives of the authorities.
If he hears something that sounds wrong, he can go to the statute itself.
For many of his dealings, he relies on a sheet that abstracts key information from each statute. It indicates which authorities must come to
him for approval of a project costing $100,000 and which must obtain
approval for a project costing $150,000; which must only *consult* with
various officers of government and which must actually obtain *approval* for various actions. The problem of this and other control
officers is that statutes differ greatly. There is no information carry-
over from one authority to another.

The simplification of statutes is one reform that might aid in the
supervision of organizations on the margins of Australia. It could help
to make each of them accountable to the same set of government
officers for similar magnitudes of expenditure; to give each authority a
chief executive and a governing board having similar powers; to estab-

lish similar procedures for approving new construction projects for each authority, or changes in the prices charged for their services. With a single map of structure and key procedures, government officers could deal with different authorities without having to become experts in the bizarre intricacies of each. Such simplification and uniformity appeal to government control officers. During Gough Whitlam's term as Prime Minister, the Commonwealth Finance Department proposed uniform components for the statutes of Commonwealth authorities, but the pressure of other work took priority. More important to most ministers was the opportunity — with a rare legislative majority for Labour — to press for new authorities. To pursue uniformity would have added another round of consultations and coordination, and put a brake on the creative process. Diversity got the better of uniformity in the short run. In the long run, the next go at uniformity must deal with the new authorities created in the wave of Whitlam legislation.

Protectionism

It is a short step from the moods of compliance and passivity in Australian statutory authorities to the use of statutes and other formal agreements to protect the status quo. Common to both the orderly acceptance of rules and the protection of an authority's market shares is an acceptance of codified opportunity and a willingness to submerge individual and corporate ambition. Protection also has other roots in Australia: it has been a common tactic of industry and organized labor; tariffs and import quotas surround Australian producers and workers; high wages, profits, and prices characterize consumer industries that operate smaller production runs than would be viable if they had to compete with the producers of North America, Japan, or Europe.

Two kinds of protectionism appear in the statutory authorities. First there is the protection of each state's interests. This has justified separate developments on either side of state frontiers out of the fear that the statutory authority of another state would discriminate against one's own residents on prices and supply of services. Thus the State Electricity Commission of Victoria developed (at great expense) its own brown coal reserves after the state found that it could not rely on supplies of more energy-efficient black coal from its neighbor state, New South Wales.[23]

The second form of protectionism seeks to limit competition between a statutory authority and a private industry. The government may freeze one or more participants at its present level of development, mandate equivalent services, or mandate that certain services cannot be offered by one or the other "competitor." Such controls may be written into the authority's statute or be incorporated in a separate agreement.

The State Bank of Victoria represents a case of protection. Restrictive clauses of its statute protect the interests of other banks. Until recently called the State Savings Bank, Victoria's State Bank limited itself to savings programs and lending for home mortgages. At one point its management gained a statutory amendment to permit checking accounts, but it still cannot offer overdrafts. It does make consumer loans, but differences in procedure lessen its appeal compared with commercial banks that make overdrafts generally available.

The best-known case of ordered competition is Australia's two-airline policy.[24] This is enforced on two carriers that provide nationwide domestic service: Trans-Australia Airlines, which is a statutory authority of the Commonwealth, and the privately owned Ansett Airways of Australia. A virtual equivalence of equipment and service is required of both airlines. The policy mandates an equal share of mail and an equal share of government travel. Each line must operate the same kind of equipment on each route, at virtually the same time. Passengers receive similar refreshments on each line: two of the same biscuits plus a choice of coffee or tea; foreign travelers are surprised to find themselves charged for soft drinks. Most flights offer no other meal service. On neither line can a traveler use one of the common international credit cards to pay for tickets.

The Commonwealth enforces this policy directly on its own carrier and indirectly on the private airline through control of import licenses for new aircraft. Both carriers must introduce the same equipment on the same routes at the same time. One carrier had to keep new planes in the hangar for several weeks until its "competitor" received identical equipment.

There is little room for competition between the two domestic airlines. They both advertise a great deal, to the benefit at least of the media and their advertising agents. Individual Australians do perceive a difference between the lines. TAA attracts greater patronage from civil servants and university personnel, who feel drawn to its status as the public carrier. Ansett has a reputation for more attractive hostesses. Each line has friends who claim for it better pilot training or maintenance, though in fact both lines have excellent safety records by international standards. They are helped in this by having better weather and less traffic than can be found on the average field in North America or Europe.

Both airlines receive their share of complaints caused by the regulated competition between them. Travelers flying between the main cities of Australia face three or four periods each day when there are double flights within minutes of one another, followed by long periods of no flights. Better schedules would open up significant opportunities for passengers. Both firms expressed interest in competitive scheduling during 1978, but the latest timetables still show identical connections between major cities.

Another aspect of passivity — and protectionism — on the margins of the Australian state is the career patterns of managers. It is difficult to find a senior official of a statutory authority who has spent his career moving upward by transferring between organizations. It is even more difficult to find a senior manager who is not a "he." Each authority is a protected male preserve surrounding junior and mid-range executives with formal or informal seniority criteria for promotion and imposing severe costs on those who leave one organization for a better job in another.

The maleness of the executive suite is bolstered by formal rules that disappeared long ago from public organizations in the United States. Some statutory authorities even force retirement on all women who marry! Reemployment is a possibility, but only as a "temporary" without rights of job protection or pension. Asked to defend such arrangements, some executives chuckle and others attack the questioner's values. "It's always been that way," is a stock answer. Still others comment on the natural place of married women in the home, or on the need to preserve high-paying jobs for male breadwinners.

Seniority is also a virtue. For many years, Victorian Railways required the use of seniority as the major criterion for promotion within executive ranks. Today seniority is the informal norm in many authorities, all but ruling out an aggressive chap who would cut ahead of the queue between him and a better job. The third-ranking officer in one major authority joined that firm as a laborer at the age of fourteen. His first step upward came via a company shorthand class, which led to a clerical position. Later he completed a high school equivalency examination and was sent by the firm to law school. This meant a job in the solicitor's department, and entry to the upper reaches of the authority. A large organization might not suffer greatly from the need to recruit senior executives from its own labor force. An organization with a work

force of over 20,000 has a high probability of finding talent somewhere in its pool. Yet this narrows advancement possibilities for individual employees. With diagonal advancement (i.e., sidewise to
another authority and upward in responsibility) blocked, talent may
wither from lack of stimulation.

An important deterrent to interorganizational mobility may appear in the authority's pension scheme. Some statutory authority pensions have little provision for transfer to or from another authority,
private industry, or government department. The financial loss en-
tailed in changing jobs can be considerably more than the salary gain,
especially when the salary gain suffers from sharply progressive tax
rates. The typical pension has one part worker's contribution, one part
interest on worker's contribution, one part employer's contribution,
and one part interest on employer's contribution. By leaving a pension
plan before retirement, an Australian typically loses all but his own
contribution. He forfeits not only his employer's contribution but also
the interest on his own contribution. He may also be charged an administrative fee for processing his withdrawal from the plan! This arrangement has all the moral appeal of Soviet efforts to bring misery to
dissidents and then charge them an administrative fee for surrendering
their citizenship.

Who Rules on the Margins?

The orderliness and stability of public life in Australia has important benefits for analysts. We can see there more clearly than in the
hurly-burly of Israel or the United States who are the major actors in
organizations on the margins of the state, and how they relate to various government officials. The picture is relatively clear in Australia
because most participants work by laws and formalized rules, and because there is so little mobility among authority personnel.

The question of who rules on the margins is important. Conventional answers invite skepticism when bodies on the margins of the state
— those purposefully given autonomy from the conventional political
process — come to be larger than the core departments of the state. In
Victoria the case may be extreme. There an estimated 84 percent of the
public sector is outside the traditional political network of control as
measured by the proportion of "public servants" working under the
Public Service Board. Recitations about the power of voters, parliamentarians, and members of the government to control public resources are highly suspect, if not obsolete, under these conditions.

Before venturing further, it is necessary to concede some limitations in the analysis. For one thing, the focus is on the State of Victoria only, not on all of Australia. The states of Australia differ among themselves, [25] and the Commonwealth government has its unique traits. The statutory authorities of Victoria, for example, are said to be less politicized than those of New South Wales, and more likely than Commonwealth authorities to recruit senior executives from within their own staffs. [26] Insofar as time and other resources limit proper research to only one Australian state, however, Victoria is a good choice. It is prominent not only in the extent of its reliance on statutory authorities but in the firm role of those authorities in the history of public services in the state. [27]

There is another problem with discussing who rules on the margins of the Australian state. Materials rely on impressions that can be illustrated by reference to particular events and conversations. Personnel at upper levels of Australian governments do not welcome close observation or detailed questioning about influence, supervision, control, or power. Some individuals are especially guarded in their comments; some do not think in terms sufficiently abstract to describe patterns in discrete events; and some have minds of great scope and flexibility and do well analyzing and participating in complex settings. Because of partial coverage and heavy reliance on inferences, the discussion that follows should be viewed as a first effort at portraying important actors on the margins of the state rather than as a detailed and widely applicable scenario.

The Chief Executive

The chief of a statutory authority is the figure most often in the center of the picture. He is likely to be the most knowledgable person and the one most likely to be involved in crucial decisions. This does not mean he dominates all decisions. When a matter is important enough to involve the Commonwealth Prime Minister or a state Premier, the head of a statutory authority is deferential. Then he is inferior in status and authority, and may be a supplicant for resources that only the Prime Minister or Premier can bestow.

In a state, the Premier may be the only one who can effectively say no to the chief officer of a major statutory authority. These chief officers are among a small number of really big boys in their state. The resources directly under their control are greater than those of virtually any department of state government. Several authorities tower over the ministries to which they are formally accountable. Neither ministers nor "permanent heads" (senior civil servants directly under a minister) approach the status enjoyed by the chief of a major authority. If one of these other actors wants to turn down a formal request from a major statutory authority, he may need the weight of the Premier to back him up.

Chief executives of major statutory authorities think and behave like politicians, although they serve in appointed positions at the pleasure of their board or the government. In private conversation, and in some official reports, they recognize explicitly the importance of their organization in state politics. They are alert to the weight of public opinion and seek to shape and schedule major actions with various groups in mind. This is especially true regarding price increases, labor relations, and the start of major projects that may attract protest groups. Authority heads often receive special requests from members of Parliament or the government. One chief executive estimates three calls a day on matters large (e.g., rate increases) or small (e.g., amenities for clients at a field office). Executives must balance the protection or promotion of their own organizations with the needs of the state politicians.

In Victoria, the State Co-ordination Council has emerged as a forum in which the chief executives of statutory authorities exercise their influence in an informal senate. The council — and its counterparts elsewhere in Australia — is designed to allow key personnel from different bodies to focus on major problems. It has as members the permanent heads of state ministries and the chiefs of major statutory authorities. In 1977 it had thirty-seven members. This made the full body too cumbersome for the attention of its real members; formal meetings attracted deputies in their place. However, the committees of the Co-ordination Council have attracted the big leaguers. Insiders report that heads of statutory authorities operate there with characteristic circumspection, but they signal that the cooperation of their organization on some matters requires the help of others — and the Premier — on other issues important to them.

In some statutory authorities there is competition over who is the real chief officer. There may be a full-time chairman of the board as well as a full-time chief executive, or director. The director may be acquainted with the technical workings of the authority, whereas the full-time chairman may be a generalist of high prestige appointed to represent the government. In other authorities the same person may be both chairman of the board *and* chief executive. In yet other cases, a full-time director may dominate a prestigious chairman who serves only part-time.

When two full-timers aspire to leadership, each may claim to be the most powerful. One director referred to his full-time chairman as a person who dealt mainly in public relations. The director claimed to formulate policy issues and said that the chairman explained policy to community and political groups. Allies of this same chairman, however, said that the director worked with details of planning and implementation and the chairman dealt with policy in contacts with the Prime Minister and Premier.

The Prime Minister and the Premier

The Commonwealth Prime Minister or the individual state's Premier is likely to be the individual with the greatest potential for influence over the margins as well as the core units of government, but the scope of his task helps limit his role.[28] The Premier of Victoria serves not only as prime minister of the state Parliament and government but also heads the Ministry of Finance. As finance minister, he allocates state tax funds and authorizes the pursuit of loans by governmental units and statutory authorities. The roles of central political figure and chief financial officer reinforce each other, and put the Premier at the core of major decisions. In practical terms, however, these powers assure that he can afford to examine only *major* decisions.

The choice of what the Premier looks at depends on understandings between him, senior officials in the state's Finance Ministry, and each authority's chief officer. Among the items the Premier probably will consider are major construction projects, changes in the percentage of the state's total borrowing that an authority pursues (a matter likely to be related to a major construction project), key personnel appointments (i.e., a new chief executive officer or chairman of the board), and major price increases to be charged for the authority's services. In all these matters there is likely to be give and take between the top levels of the statutory authority and the state government. When the chief officer of a statutory authority perceives that the Premier will resist a proposal, he will prepare alternative positions acceptable to the authority. For example, if a price increase must be reduced for political reasons, or delayed until after an election, the authority may seek a compensatory increase in its borrowing authority, some adjustment in the internal financing it receives from the state government, or an increase in prices charged to government entities.

After the senior officers of the authorities and the Premier, senior professionals in the Finance Ministry are the most important policy makers with respect to statutory authorities. Their influence lies in the staff work they do for the Premier, and when the Premier is not involved directly, in their exercise of routine financial control over statutory authorities. Procedures for borrowing, governmental subsidies, and sometimes price changes go through the Finance Ministry. For most of the smaller authorities, and for less important decisions of larger authorities, these controls represent the principal points of supervision by the government. Decisions of intermediate magnitude would receive close attention from the permanent head of the Finance Ministry, whereas matters of great importance would go from him to the Premier. The determination of who should make the final decision can be a matter of give and take. Major changes in borrowing, prices, and subsidy would be targeted from the start for the permanent head and the Premier. Lesser matters might reach those levels if the executives of a statutory authority or Finance personnel found special reasons to dig in their heels and insist on a particular position.

The Minister

Each unit on the margins of the Australian state is responsible to an elected minister of the government. A minister may have legal responsibility for approving major contracts, appointments of key personnel, or changes in certain policies. While the link is usually formidable in statutory terms, it is typically weak in practice. When participants are asked about the role of ministers (excluding the Premier), they usually respond in euphemisms like "He stays on top of our major problems," "We keep him informed of each step in major decisions," or "He shows close interest." Generally these comments mean a passive role for the minister. He deals episodically with items of his own personal interest, or he may be called on by the chief officer of an authority to support its needs in public, in the cabinet, or in the parliamentary party caucus. Ministers like to cultivate an image of being involved. They appear at ceremonial openings of new facilities, or at the retirement of key personnel. They announce major appointments and new contracts. They may take a posture in major labor negotiations, while leaving the details of bargaining to the professional staff and chief officer of the authority. According to one professional in a government department, the ministers "are all good fellows. They do well at the country and suburban pubs, but lack the acumen to deal with the statutory authorities."

Ministers express their own roles in homely terms. One person with a long record as minister-in-charge of major authorities expressed confidence in "his" management teams. Items that have interested him personally are working conditions on the authorities' properties within his own parliamentary constituency and simple issues that have struck his fancy. He once urged the employment of a landscape architect by an authority having trouble with citizen protests against its unsightly facilities. "It was the simplest thing," he reports, "to put the damn things behind the hills rather than on top of the hills.... For a little extra money we saved a lot of criticism."

Ministers refrain from more intensive involvement with their statutory authorities by limiting the size of their staffs. One works with a ministry of 9 employees, including clerical and secretarial personnel, that has nominal control over statutory organizations with staffs approaching 20,000 people. Another ministry that identifies itself as aggressive in dealings with statutory authorities has a staff of 30; its authorities employ some 35,000. One minister allows major statutory authorities to bypass his department's permanent head and bring matters to him directly. This minister leaves himself with no advice contrary to that received from the authorities.

The Permanent Head

The case of a statutory authority's bypassing a ministry's permanent head makes a telling point about the relative weight of actors from the margins and the core units of government. In traditional theory, permanent heads are the great figures of the civil service: they are senior professionals who report directly to a minister; they are the minister's principal source of policy advice; and they bridge the gap between the civil service and the government. They receive the highest salaries offered to members of the civil service, frequently participate in the most prestigious clubs of Australia's capital cities, and aspire to knighthood. Yet in a quiet power play the chief executives of two statutory authorities decided between themselves and the minister that a permanent head was not up to the supervision of their activities. They claimed he lacked familiarity with the details of their industry. At least part of the problem was one of protocol and bureaucratic politics. The permanent head had been recruited from another state, and the selection committee that chose him, organized by the Public Service Board, had failed to consult the chiefs of these authorities. The Public Service Board sees itself as representative and guardian of the permanent heads and other elite civil servants, and it may have wanted to stick something to up-start statutory authorities. The Public Service Board could prevail in the short run; formal procedures permit, but do not require, consulta-tion with statutory authorities on a matter of choosing a permanent head. In the longer run, the big statutory authorities had enough clout to bypass a permanent head they did not participate in selecting.

Permanent heads differ among themselves in the postures they take with respect to authorities. Ostensibly, they participate in the legal power ministers hold over authorities. Permanent heads can direct staff personnel to study issues raised by the authorities, and then summarize a departmental position for the minister's consideration. Yet at least one permanent head seems content with a token staff that renders him incompetent in the face of proposals and analyses from statutory au-thorities. He does not seem to perceive the possibility of a greater role. He claims that statutes give certain prerogatives over his department to the authorities when, in fact, the statutes do not grant these rights.

Another permanent head has been aggressive in seeking to increase his control over the statutory authorities. While this man concedes that "his" statutory authorities have the greater weight, he has sought to expand and strengthen his departmental staff. His strategy is not to compete directly with authority analyses on every issue, but to probe deeply enough into their proposals to force them to more thorough justifications for their major ventures. This permanent head is more calculating and aggressive than the typical Australian official. He once sought to change the name of his department in order to rid it of a neg-ative stereotype acquired during a previous regime. He centralized public announcements and conversations with the media in his hands and those of the minister. He tried to change one authority's programs by recruiting an outsider to serve in a key position. He views his own position as in natural competition with the statutory authorities, and describes his advantages and weaknesses with respect to the tactics pursued by authorities to keep decisions in their own hands: "They'll call something 'technical' when it's really a matter of general policy." He sees no mileage for his department in labor relations and thus leaves them to the authorities and the minister. This permanent head expresses deferential attitudes toward his minister, but also laments the minister's practice of shifting his attention from one issue to another. The need to keep up with these shifts gets in the way of pursuing some issues far enough to master an authority on its own terrain. He admits to short-circuiting some procedures of the Public Service Board in order to increase his staff. He recognizes some danger to his position in certain tactics, yet he balances these risks with a careful appraisal of what he receives from the effort. In his mind, it results in somewhat greater capacity to turn back for further review, or even to turn down, the proposals of giant authorities.

The Public Service Board

The Public Service Board has nominal responsibility over the selection, remuneration, and promotion of state employees in Victoria. The emphasis should be on *nominal*, for only 16 percent of all public servants come directly under its wing. Like other core government units, the Public Service Board has attenuated as units on the margins have grown. The board seeks to maintain the status and other privileges of the conventional public service in competition with personnel on the margins. The Public Service Board is something like the dog being wagged by its tail, or the former insider now on the outside. The chairman and two other members of the board work on various interdepartmental or cabinet-level committees to keep salaries in the statutory authorities in line with those in the conventional public service. Salaries of authority chief executives are pegged to those of permanent heads in the conventional departments, taking into consideration the number of employees in the various authorities and departments. This means that chief executives of the largest authorities, like Victorian Railways and the State Electricity Commission, receive more money than most of the permanent heads in government departments.

Members and employees of the Public Service Board express some ambivalence toward the statutory authorities. One employee questioned whether it was still true that the policies of the authorities "and not the departments make up the fast-moving current in Victorian politics."[29] Yet a more senior colleague conceded that neither ministers nor departmental staff can compete with the executives of the statutory authorities in setting policies.

The permanent heads are the major reference group of the Public Service Board. When board members say that they aim to serve "our customers," they mean the permanent heads. The Public Service Board advertises for vacancies at the level of permanent heads, and convenes selection teams to screen applicants. The board seeks to protect the status of permanent heads in policy making as well as in salary and perquisites. Recent challenges to the position of the permanent heads have come from a new breed of employees, the private secretaries of ministers. Each minister is allowed two or three secretarial appointments to handle such chores as public relations, clerical work, and the handling of constituency service. Until recently the ministers lacked any formal aides they could call their own. Now the Public Service Board perceives some private secretaries asserting themselves. Some ministers have relied on the policy advice of personal secretaries rather than on their permanent heads. Some private secretaries, despite their youth, have been considered by ministers as appropriate replacements for a permanent head about to retire. Such attitudes are threatening to a status-loaded bureaucracy tilted in favor of its senior members. The Public Service Board has moved in defense of its "customers" by keeping the salaries of private secretaries low enough to discourage any but the youngest applicants. The board uses its role in the selection process for permanent heads to reinforce criteria of age and long service for those positions. Board members have also helped educate ministers to the traditional role of the permanent head as principal adviser and channel for the expertise of the civil service.

Some Authorities Are More Equal Than Others

In seeking to understand the margins of the Australian state, it is important to note that attitudes and behaviors of government officials differ toward various authorities. The size of an authority has much to do with this. An authority with a large staff or a large annual claim on state borrowing, or one that deals with a large number of clients, receives more careful treatment than a small body that works in a narrow field of the state's economy. The State Electricity Commission, Victorian Railways, and the Melbourne and Metropolitan Board of Works receive more attention than the Grain Elevators Board or the Victorian Dried Fruits Board.

Even among the important authorities, there are variations in the quality of their treatment by government officials. There is room for bureaucratic discretion and political clout. Victorian Railways has long been vulnerable to demands that it provide services that are not commercially viable, and the state Parliament has tolerated substantial annual losses. Bureaucratic insiders do not regard highly Vic Rail's accounts or its capacity to justify requests. The 1977-78 loss of Vic Rail increased by $11 million from the year before, to $152.3 million. And this was the first time in the decade that the loss was within the annual budget projections of the state government. Another low-status body is the Housing Commission. At the height of the 1977 inquiry into the commission's land scandal, one government officer said of its presentations, "We don't believe anything they say. We look as closely as we can." Contrasted with this is the status of the State Electricity Commission of Victoria. Its reputation is for strong and sophisticated leadership. One senior official in the state government pointed to an article written by the chairman of the SEC and praised it for presenting cost information far superior to that of other enterprises.[30] Another officer said, "If I were to refuse one of the SEC requests they'd send an army in here." He meant an army of analysts capable of justifying requests at a level of detail he could not challenge. Even the SEC has come in for hard times, however, as the priorities of the state population have changed. Now the concern is not solely for an assured supply of electricity at any price. Environmental considerations have come to the fore to delay or deter such SEC projects as the location of high-tension lines or the expansion of generating plants.

Some enterprises do well in the government on the basis of their political clout. This may come from their pursuit of goals widely shared by the public and the state Premier, or because they have the patronage of a minister who shows more than the usual aggression and skill in pushing a case within the government. While Vic Rail is a target for close examination by state bureaucrats, its friends in the state Parliament demand rail service in their constituencies and often tolerate financial losses.

Until 1978 the Melbourne and Metropolitan Board of Works had a peculiar structure that brought politics right into the boardroom and made government control awkward. Its statute gave a seat on the board to every local authority in the metropolitan area, and led to a fair amount of horse trading in the selection of projects. The staff of MMBW, as well as government control units, found board actions hard to take, but harder to resist. One executive spoke for much of the professional management when he testified at an inquiry about the desirability of reducing the size and functions of the board. Such a proposal echoed the sentiments of many participants and observers of board activities. Although the formal inquiry of 1977 began in response to some members of local councils who chafed at the leadership of Alan Croxford as board chairman, the inquiry ended by reducing the role of local councils in the board's makeup and with the reappointment of Croxford to a new term as chairman.

There is some buck-passing from Victoria control units in the case of state enterprises that operate with special project grants from Canberra. The state government is disinclined to deal forcefully with the financing of sewage programs by the Board of Works, hospital projects by the Hospitals and Charities Commission, or housing schemes by the Housing Commission.

The State Bank touches many residents as the largest home mortgage lender in the state. Yet it seems to attract less direct supervision from the Premier or the state Finance Ministry than other bodies of comparable size. This is partly because the State Bank is profitable and does not claim any government resources and partly because its activities are monitored routinely along with those of private banks.

The landscape of Australian public enterprise is occasionally relieved by unconventional aggression. The head of one firm that competes with private enterprise outlined a series of steps taken to improve his firm's position and spoke with pride about its dominance in several sectors of the market. When asked if he wanted to be the biggest firm in his field, he responded with a glint in his eye that he wanted to be the *only* firm. The head of an enterprise in Western Australia took a permissive view of his statute: "If the law doesn't prohibit something, I'll go ahead and do it." With this reasoning he used some profits to purchase a printing firm to produce the forms he needed to deal with the public; in conjunction with firms in the private sector, he bought a radio station when he could not get sufficient notice in the media for his services; and he parlayed surplus computer facilities into a profitable consulting subsidiary.

Authority Executives
as Distinctive Personalities

The chiefs of statutory authorities also differ in their political roles. As a group, these people have eclipsed the permanent heads of government departments as major policy makers, and they have left the ministers (except for the Premier) and backbench members of Parliament with attenuated positions in electoral politics. Yet, like all groups of importance, there is much to learn from variations among the members. If political scientists want to understand how policies are made and resources distributed from the margins of the state, we had better drop our preoccupation with conventional actors and look to this new group.

Victoria offers two extreme models from its collection of statutory authorities. Although they do not exhaust the features of personality and behavior to be found on the margins of the Australian state, they present interesting materials for the beginning of analysis. These two executives differ not only on the surface but also because their differences reflect the structures and the missions of their organizations.

The figures are J. Charles Trethowan, chairman and chief executive officer of the State Electricity Commission of Victoria, and Alan Croxford, chairman of the Melbourne and Metropolitan Board of Works. Both have great weight in their realms and dominate their organizations. While both are politically astute, Trethowan's style is that of a *technocrat*, whereas Croxford is more overtly a *politico*.

J. Charles Trethowan is an accountant-economist by training who climbed from the ranks of employed professionals to the executive suite of the State Electricity Commission. His personal manner is modest but confident. He is articulate in speech and on paper. He has contributed to an academic journal of public administration and is a frequent participant in training programs for upper-level managers in the public and private sectors. He is an accomplished organizer of personnel and argument. His program analyses and proposals are cited as models by key control officers in the government.

Associates of Trethowan cite him as the possessor of one of the sharpest political minds in Victoria, and praise his gentleness of manner that belies the power he wields. Trethowan's own assessments of antagonists and allies are trenchant. A formal report to members of his board and the state cabinet after the costly strike of 1977 was balanced and delicate in conceding the quality of labor leaders, and in citing political leaders for their failure to involve themselves more deeply before the strike reached a crisis. Trethowan has a firm understanding of his role in political matters. Like leaders of electric power firms in other developed countries, he expects the SEC to receive continuing pressure from environmentalists, from other public bodies that covet the economic resources it demands, from restive workers, and from occasional extremists. In the midst of conflict he is sensitive about the substance of his actions and about public relations. He attends to the message and the media. He prepares impressive justifications and multiple fallback positions for each major session with the state Finance Ministry or the Premier. He seeks to meet the arguments of labor or environmentalists with an insistence on formal procedure and a thorough documentation for the commission's position.

Alan Croxford differs from Charles Trethowan on several dimensions. Croxford has a reputation for personal flamboyance, and for being in the thick of political controversy. Where Trethowan wins disputes by the logic of his presentation, Croxford seems to rely on the weight of coalition. Colorful allegations about Croxford pass among people claiming to be insiders. As a result of his numerous enemies and the widespread gossip, he has been the target of two official inquiries. Neither produced sufficient evidence to provoke his dismissal, much less his indictment. Indeed, shortly after the second inquiry recommended a major change in the structure of the Melbourne and Metropolitan Board of Works, the state government appointed Alan Croxford as the first chairman of the reformed organization.

Both Charles Trethowan and Alan Croxford are partly the creatures of their organizations. Trethowan's skill as a technocrat fits into the tradition of the State Electricity Commission; most SEC chiefs have been professional engineers preoccupied with proposals prepared and justified on technical criteria.[31] The SEC is organized as a hierarchy, with a single head who combines the functions of chairman of the board and chief executive officer. Now that the source of electricity is contentious, and the people of Victoria are not content simply with supporting material progress without reference to its social or aesthetic costs, the technocrat in charge must add public relations to his quiver of skills. Trethowan approaches meetings with the press and citizen groups with the same attention to detail that he and his predecessors have always shown when they approached the state Premier.

Alan Croxford came to lead an organization that is explicitly political. Initially one of fifty-four local councilors, he was chosen by the Doncaster-Templestone municipal council to represent it on the Board of Works. Croxford rose to the board's chairmanship by his skill in putting together coalitions necessary to enact policies dealing with matters close to the heart of people in Melbourne and its suburbs. The board's activities in town planning plus water and sewer services determine which land will be available for development; such power can make fortunes for real estate speculators or freeze a site for years without chance of profit. The board also determines the amount of land available for residents, which affects the price of home ownership for thousands of families each year. Land dealing has long been a vehicle of speculation in Melbourne. Melbourne has a history of men who have mixed private aims with public authority, as revealed in the 1977 inquiry into the Housing Commission.[32] Policies of the Board of Works are usually contentious. Losers have been quick to get angry at winners, and quick to charge sharp or dirty dealing.

Croxford's position at the center of all this is exaggerated by the centrality of the Board of Works in local government in the Melbourne area. The board's function is without parallel in any U.S. metropolitan area. This body, with a single visible figure at its head, is responsible for land-use control across the fifty-one municipalities of the metropolis. The reality of his job has required that Croxford be a wheeler and dealer among shifting coalitions of the board. How else would he get majority approvals for decisions bound to award benefits and costs unequally from one community to another or one property owner to another? Moreover, Croxford's skill in staying on top of such an organization for more than a decade virtually assures him of enemies. The truth of allegations about him must escape our attention; this book is not an exercise in investigative journalism or a substitute for formal inquiries by the state government of Victoria. Yet the lack of formal citation against Croxford after two official inquiries is impressive in itself. It testifies to his skill as a politician, just as the persistence of allegations testifies to the overtly political nature of his position.

MANAGERIAL CONTROL
AND POLITICAL ACCOUNTABILITY

On both management control and political accountability, the statute is a critical link between the core departments and margins of the Australian state. With precision and frequent amendments, Australian government officials and managers of statutory authorities make public details of programs and procedures of accountability. Officials and citizens can learn what the authorities should be accomplishing and how their officers should be checked by government.

The problem comes at the point of using the statutes. Too many giants are on the margins of the Australian state, and the statutes meant to control them are too individualized to serve as effective means of control. That it all hangs together, most of the time, reflects in great measure voluntary compliance. It could not work without Australians' conservative view of what law permits: that an action must be explicitly permitted and not only authorized by silence. If entrepreneurship were more prevalent in Australia, the statutory means of control would most likely fail. The statutes are skeletons without strong organs of enforcement. They are like an unguarded fat goose waiting to be snatched, which is safe because almost all the neighborhood boys are too decent to take advantage.

In the next chapter we shall see the need for the national and local governments to create strong monitoring bodies to supervise public-sector entrepreneurs. In Israel, the Treasury and other ministries, the

State Comptroller, and the ombudsmen have larger staffs, and they are more distrusting and more aggressive than their Australian counterparts. Lest any Israeli idealize Australia's reliance on statutes as simple and effective controls over the margins of the state, let him not forget the passive and law-abiding political culture that underlies the Australian statutes. If Israel were to adopt the Australian pattern, she would risk repeating on a sociopolitical plane the Australian experience with rabbits and blackberries. The entrepreneurs of Israel's government-owned companies would have a field day with government controllers who relied on statutes alone. Israeli managers need aggressive government controllers.

As a conclusion to this chapter, a focus on the operation of the Australian model in the Australian setting must say that, most of the time, the results seem to be adequate. There are few aggressive entrepreneurs in the public sector of Australia. One chairman of a statutory authority took pleasure in reciting a list of achievements going back over his tenure. Each achievement was one more advantage he acquired by way of statutory amendment that gave his organization more opportunities to compete with private firms operating in the same sector of the economy. The chief executive of another authority noted how he used some profits from his principal line of business to purchase firms in other fields. He expressed a view of law often heard in Israel and the United States, but unusual in Australia: "If the law doesn't prohibit something, I'll go ahead and do it."

Such incidents of entrepreneurship seem to have exploited the normal passivity of government controllers for the benefit of public authorities. Other incidents of Australian entrepreneurship have sought private benefit. The land scandal of the Victoria Housing Commission is the best recent example; behavior of a kind nurtured in Boston, New York, or Chicago found easy pickings in Melbourne. That these incidents are exceptions justifies the usual pursuit, in Australia, of managerial control and political accountability via explicit statutes and assumptions of voluntary compliance.

3

ISRAEL:
ENTREPRENEURIAL
MANAGERS
ON
THE
MARGINS

Sharp contrasts exist between the margins of the State of Israel and those of the Australian states. Australian culture is passive, and its managers usually comply with statutes that define their activities. This chapter highlights the unfettered entrepreneurialism of Israel. A glut of organizations mix government and private ownership in all fields of the economy. Continuous jousting takes place between managers of government companies who seek independence and government officials who devise new procedures for supervision and control.

Public and private life in Israel is a cacophony of noise, tension, high emotions, and continuous movement of people not satisfied with their present lot or their organizations. The term *balagan* characterizes the confusion that hyperactivity brings to private households and public offices alike. Witty Israelis say that Jews are just like other people, only more so. Israel, too, is just like other countries, only more so.

It is difficult to find an Israeli manager who has stayed with one firm for an entire career. Men and women seek opportunity through mobility. I once met the deputy mayor of a large municipality in the morning; that evening, he was on television as the spokesman for a major government company. Later I learned that he was trying this out as a second job to see how he liked it.

Public organizations are everywhere. They deal not only with power generation, transportation, water provision, and the exploitation of minerals but cover manufacturing, construction, wholesaling and retailing, agricultural production, distribution, and export. Often public bodies compete in the same field. The government deals in housing through several mortgage banks and construction firms, each claiming to handle a distinctive slice of the market. A new government housing firm appeared recently, created by an entrepreneur who persuaded the cabinet Committee on the Economy that he had discovered a slice of the market not served adequately. His firm prepares plans and infrastructure for raw land and then leases it to small private contractors for residential and commercial construction.

THE LAND, THE PEOPLE, AND THE GOVERNMENT

The land of Israel has been a cradle and a crossroads. The Jewish people developed there, and today some 25 percent of the world's Jews live in the old-new State of Israel. Historically the land has been a point of contention. The Israeli locality of Magiddo (Armaggedon) reveals in more than twenty layers of settlement—each destroyed on top of preceding ruins—what occurred at a historic junction of major highways. This is where the ancient route from Egypt to Phoenicia (Lebanon) branches off to Damascus.

Israel is a small place—some 8,000 square miles prior to the 1967 war—about midway between the size of New Jersey and Massachusetts. It is always necessary to specify which concept of Israel is at issue, usually in relation to one or another war. Its location is physically in the heart of the Middle East, where Eurasia and Africa come together. Because of the animosity of its neighbors and the cultural background of many of its inhabitants, however, Israel orients much of its commerce toward Europe. Its governmental structures and processes also have European roots.

The large majority of Israelis share a Jewish identity but differ in ways that reflect their wanderings across much of the world. They trace themselves or their parents to a hundred countries, with major contingents from such widely scattered places as Yemen, Iraq, Iran, Morocco, Poland, Romania, and the Soviet Union. Some Jewish families go back to medieval or biblical times in Israel, and a majority of Jewish residents were born in Israel and speak Hebrew as their mother tongue. Yet cultural diversity remains an important feature of the Israeli scene.

The government of Israel is a parliamentary democracy along the model found in most Western European countries. There is a single-house parliament, the Knesset, elected on the basis of proportional representation. A dozen or so parties compete in a single nationwide constituency. Each party offers a ranked list of candidates and places as many candidates in the Knesset as the party receives a percentage of the popular vote. A figurehead President is head of state, and a Prime Minister heads the government. No party has ever received a simple majority; since the independence of modern Israel in 1948, every government has been a coalition. For this reason, the Prime Minister, usually the leader of the largest party, may not be a strong leader. He or she may have little actual discretion given the power of each partner in the coalition.

The government of Israel includes the Prime Minister plus such other ministries as Finance, Defense, Foreign Affairs, Agriculture, Commerce and Industry, Transportation, Education, Welfare, Interior, Health, Housing, Tourism, and Religious Affairs. Each minister's portfolio may vary from one government to the next, according to the demands of leading politicians and their negotiations with the Prime Minister. Attached to most ministries are limited-liability companies (similar to American corporations) that are the most prominent bodies on the margins of the Israeli state.

The beleaguered nature of Israel has left several marks on its government. The high cost of the defense budget plus the commitment of most Israelis to maintain a full-service welfare state results in a tax burden that may be the highest in the world. In this connection it is important to note that one or another labor-socialist party dominated government coalitions from independence in 1948 to the election of 1977, when the Likud party of Prime Minister Menachem Begin emerged with the most votes — but without a majority.

Another indication of Israel's beleaguered nature is the preoccupation of most governments with defense and foreign policies; few Prime Ministers have devoted their energies to domestic institutions or programs. Israelis can find much to reform in their public services, but major change is not in the cards as long as defense remains such a high priority.

THE STATE OF ISRAEL

The very definitions of the Israeli government and its margins become blurred in the variety of public institutions. Numerous companies are owned wholly or partly by the national government and subordinate entities like municipalities. Other companies belong wholly or partly to the Histadrut, the Labor Federation, which is legally and organizationally distinct from the government but is tied to it by numerous joint ventures and much overlap in personnel. Some people transfer from one entity to the other; some hold positions simultaneously in the ruling circles of both. There are also companies owned wholly or in part by the Jewish Agency and other institutions of the international Jewish community. These may be formally responsible to international organizations like the World Zionist Organization, which is governed by delegates elected by Jewish organizations of different countries and is financed from contributions raised abroad and from the profits of firms operating in Israel. The bodies of international Jewry are, like the Histadrut, distinct from the State of Israel. Nevertheless, they engage in joint ventures with the government and the Histadrut. Leading officers of international Jewish organizations, whether they are formally Israelis or not, are important figures in the public life of Israel. Other public bodies, such as universities, also own companies that engage in joint ventures with the government.

Officers of the government have certain controls over the activities of companies owned by the Histadrut, the Jewish Agency, and other public bodies, as well as over those owned by the Israeli state. Personnel in the Finance Ministry and other ministries have had to issue permits for transfers of currency or loan commitments, and licenses to build certain facilities. Often a company of the Histadrut or the Jewish Agency will come to the Ministry of Commerce and Industry for a subsidy to encourage the development of industry in new towns. This gives the government some leverage over those institutions not technically part of it.

The familial or tribal nature of Israeli Jewish society also helps weld disparate organizations more closely than at first sight. Generations ago, founders of the government, the Histadrut, and the Jewish Agency came out of the same social strata and youth groups of Eastern Europe. The next generation fought together in the Haganah or another of the underground armies during the period of the British Mandate. The current generation of managers had common experiences in school, scouts, the Israeli Army, and political parties. Career patterns show movement between offices of the government, the Histadrut, and the Jewish Agency. In a small country, networks of friends and family fill in the gaps not covered by common experiences. The result of all this is considerable confusion as to where the government ends and other public organizations begin. A legal craftsman can define the boundaries of the State of Israel as they exclude the Histadrut and institutions of the international Jewish community; a sociologist would have greater difficulty.

THE MARGINS OF THE STATE

For the purposes of this book, any effort to define the margins of the Israeli state must reckon with different layers that have developed in Israel. In our terms, the margins stretch beyond institutions responsible to the government per se. They include institutions of the Histadrut, the Jewish Agency, and other public bodies, as well as joint ventures involving at least one of these owners.

The nature of the terrain complicates management and political accountability. Formal lines of control originate not only in government offices but also in the ruling councils of the Labor Federation and the World Zionist Organization. Formal and informal channels cross from one superior body to the other — dealing not only with joint ventures but with frequent discussions and negotiations about national economic or social policy. *Management by whom?* and *political accountability to whom?* are questions to be begged in the short run; they will be addressed later in this chapter, after more attention to details. Even then, the complexity will frustrate any effort to paint a picture as clear as that of Australia, for the incoherence of Israel challenges description and analysis. By starting with Australia, we dealt with the easiest task first.

Government Companies

It is difficult even to count the units on the margins of the Israeli state. Starting with companies owned by the government, we find two competing definitions of a government company. The first, which appears in the law of the Government Companies Authority, identifies a government company as one with at least 50 percent government ownership or 50 percent government participation in its direction. The State Comptroller, an agent of the Knesset, operates under a second law, which places in its jurisdiction all companies with some government ownership or some government role in their direction. A recent annual report of the Government Companies Authority records 105 entities that are "government companies" by its definition; the State Comptroller has not recently toted up the number of government companies by its calculations. Neither the Government Companies Authority nor the State Comptroller has added up the subsidiaries of government companies or the joint ventures between government and private owners. There are an additional 120 companies owned by municipalities. These are nominally tied to the government because municipal authorities derive in direct line from the Interior Ministry. Neither the Interior Ministry nor the Finance Ministry seems sure who is responsible for municipally owned companies.

Jerusalem owns twelve corporations, Tel Aviv twenty-seven, and Haifa six; seventy-five others are owned by lesser cities, towns, and regional councils. Municipalities join in these firms with partners from the Israeli state, the Histadrut, the Jewish Agency, companies owned by these bodies, other public agencies, and private investors. Municipal firms include savings and mortgage banks, land developers, builders, theaters, museums, sports stadiums, and companies that supply water and build roads.[1]

Companies of the government include some giants in the Israeli economy. Israel Aviation Industries employs over 16,000 workers and produces internationally attractive commercial aircraft, fighter planes, and naval patrol boats. El Al is the flag carrier in international aviation. Israel Chemical is a holding company for subsidiaries that exploit the various minerals of the Dead Sea and the Negev. Banks owned by the government deal in mortgages for immigrants and young couples, industrial investment, and financial aid to industries involved in exports. Israel Coins and Medals Corporation, a company with only sixty employees, produces commemorative coins and medals in gold, silver, and bronze that have won favor among international collectors. This company earned an after-tax profit of 27 percent for the government in 1974-75, but it also attracted the attention of the State Comptroller, who exposed certain improprieties in its management.[2]

Ministers create companies, or assign tasks to them rather than to agencies within their departments, for several reasons. Ministers may ask a company to pay for something that will not fit within the government budget. Or a minister can use a company to dodge responsibility for a risky project. If it succeeds, the minister takes credit; if it fails, the minister cites the autonomy of the company and claims the project was outside his control.

Some companies tackle projects that carry political or legal problems that would deter government. An example is the sports stadium proposed for Jerusalem. A company owned partly by the municipality might succeed in building a stadium in the vicinity of a religious neighborhood in spite of protests about noise and heavy traffic on the Sabbath. A department of the municipality could not handle the project at all, because of the religious parties on the city council.

Companies are useful in absorbing personnel. A tired manager can be moved from a ministry to a company sinecure. A deserving party member can be given a soft job or a real challenge in a company, depending on circumstances.

Each year the government buys and sells shares of companies. Some companies pass from majority to minority government control or the reverse. Some of this share trading reflects the opportunity to sell part of a company to a private investor; this helps the Finance Ministry in its quest for a smaller deficit or the Bank of Israel in its pursuit of foreign currency. On the other hand, the government's purchase of shares is a way to provide new capital, to get a project off the ground, or to keep a shaky company from going under. When the Likud government came to power in 1977, it was committed to a smaller role for the government and more free enterprise. A hotshot deputy minister of finance promised to liquidate government holdings in numerous companies. Yet company personnel resist drastic changes, and many of Israel's socialists oppose such policy in principle. Also, the stock market of a small country can absorb only so many shares. After a year and a half in office, the Likud government had only one company on its *For Sale* list. It could not sell significantly more shares than had the overtly socialist governments of the Labor party.

The Histadrut

The Histadrut is involved in some two thousand companies.[3] Yet the relationship of the Histadrut with these companies can vary greatly from one to another. Some companies are owned wholly or largely by a division of the Histadrut called Workers' Companies. These include Koor Industries, a conglomerate of heavy and consumer industry firms that appears on *Fortune* magazine's list of the five hundred largest corporations in the world. There is also the Workers' Housing Company, one of Israel's largest builders of residential housing, not all of it restricted to the working class. The Histadrut also owns the Workers' Bank, the second largest in the country, with branches in virtually every urban neighborhood and rural community. Also in the financial sector there are Histadrut pension funds that serve not only workers of Histadrut industries but the private sector, public institutions like universities and hospitals, and government companies (but not the civil service per se). The extensive coverage of these pension schemes distinguishes Israel from Australia and facilitates a high level of managerial mobility from one Israeli organization to another.

Somewhat different in its relationship to the Labor Federation is its Sick Fund. This grouping of clinics, pharmacies, hospitals, rest homes, physicians, nurses, therapists, and other related services is the Histadrut's principal tie to many of its members. Three quarters of Israel's population belongs to the Histadrut and receives low-cost benefits from its Sick Fund. However, the government subsidy that permits the Sick Fund to operate at low membership dues gives an important voice in Sick Fund policies to the Finance and Health ministries.

Also linked to the Histadrut, but not owned by it, are various cooperatives including agricultural cooperatives — kibbutzim and moshavim — that account for a majority of Israel's agricultural production. These cooperatives in turn own industrial and service companies and are grouped into organizations that operate banks, purchasing entities, and marketing companies. Also linked to the Histadrut are two bus cooperatives that provide most of the public land transportation in the country. These bus cooperatives depend heavily on the government for subsidies, licenses, and permits.

In its overall structure the Histadrut resembles a government. Indeed, the Histadrut is older than the State of Israel by twenty-eight years, and it resists occasional moves to subordinate its units to those of the nation. Political parties affiliated with those in the government arena compete in nationwide elections for places on the national council of the Histadrut, whose executive and judicial units resemble their counterparts in the government. Major units that answer to the chief executive of the Histadrut (the General Secretary) include a Trade Union Department, the holding company for Histadrut enterprises (Workers' Companies), social security and mutual aid organizations, a Department of International Relations, a Women's Council, an Arab Workers Department, and a Unit for Cultural and Educational Organization (responsible for Histadrut vocational and higher education institutions, youth movements, sports clubs, and daily newspapers in Hebrew and Arabic). All told, Histadrut firms account for some 23 percent of the employment in Israel and 20 percent of net product.[4] The greater percentage of employment than production reveals the traditional Histadrut concern with providing work, in keeping with its role as the federation of Israeli labor unions.

Issues of principle as well as profit swirl within and outside the Histadrut. This is no surprise in a labor federation that manages companies, operates a wide range of social services, and represents workers. Histadrut companies enter partnerships with private investors as well as with the government, the Jewish Agency, and municipalities. There is explicit concern about the social mission of Histadrut holdings and mechanisms to involve workers' committees in company management. Yet there are wildcat strikes by workers who claim that the Histadrut has lost sight of their needs, for example, when the Histadrut joins with government on policies of wage restraint. There is also a continuing debate about the essential character of the Histadrut: whether it is a proper form of socialism or a variety of labor plus government capitalism.[5]

The Jewish Agency

There are special problems in compiling a list of companies owned by the Jewish Agency, for the agency is sensitive to outsiders and operates with formal canons of secrecy. This posture dates back to the days when it worked for the illegal immigration of Jews through the British blockade, helped to scour the depots of Europe for war materiel to be purchased through third parties, and arranged for the departure of Jews and their property from countries with closed borders. Contemporary Jewish Agency officials are as open as other Israelis, however, even though they hold to official confidentiality. They cannot let an outsider see a list of agency companies, but they illustrate their comments with references to a variety of companies in which they admit the agency owns some or many shares.

Many Jewish Agency companies show the influence of the agency's concern with immigration and economic and social development. There are companies that build homes for immigrants, industrial workshops that provide employment in country towns and small cities, a sheltered workshop for the handicapped, and banks that provide mortgages and small loans to immigrants. The agency acquired a minority shareholdership in El Al Airlines when that firm was heavily involved in airlifting immigrants to Israel. The agency bought a piece of the *Jerusalem Post* when the English-language daily was in danger of going under. Among the agency's holdings is Bank Leumi, which traces its lineage to a bank established by Theodore Herzl. It has become the largest bank in the country and one of the largest in the world, with branches stretching eastward to Melbourne and westward to Los Angeles.

Wits speculate that the Jewish Agency will not let outsiders see its list of companies because no such list exists. In fact, the organizational structures above and below Jewish Agency headquarters are complex enough to trouble any specialist in administrative engineering. Lines of control and definitions of who does what would compete well in international competitions for incoherence. Introspective persons at the highest levels of the agency admit to the confusion that surrounds them.

The World Zionist Organization is a major actor in the government of the Jewish Agency. The WZO itself is governed by delegates elected from organizations in Israel and sixty-eight other countries. WZO's board of trustees, president, board of directors, and director general govern Keren Hayesod, a fund-raising and social service organization for communities outside the United States. The Jewish communities in the United States have their own organization, the United Jewish Appeal. Partly because of U.S. government regulations pertaining to contributions that can be deducted from taxable incomes, the United Jewish Appeal retains control over its own activities. The Jewish Agency is careful to segregate UJA money from Israeli government funds and programs in Israel. The Jewish Agency, in turn, is responsible to the Jewish Agency Assembly, whose members are chosen 50 percent by the WZO, 30 percent by Keren Hayesod, and 20 percent by the UJA. The picture is clouded further by the influence of Jewish Agency leaders in both the World Zionist Organization and Keren Hayesod.[6]

Major divisions of the Jewish Agency deal with immigration, social welfare, health, education, housing, agriculture, and youth care. Responsibility for the various companies of the Jewish Agency is dispersed through these divisions. The Jewish Agency is currently trying to rationalize its corporate properties. Officers are compiling a list of shareholdings and considering the sale of shares in companies that no longer serve a principal social or economic mission of the agency. Persons in the Jewish Agency's Company Authority hope that the agency may use its control over companies in an integrated, policy-oriented manner. This unit is still small, however, and must feel its way in the bureaucratic maze of the Jewish Agency and related bodies of the World Zionist Organization.

The agency's connection with Bank Leumi is sufficiently complex to confuse insiders as well as outsiders. The Jewish Agency has a controlling block of shares, but the bank is actually administered through a board of directors of prestigious national figures that is self-perpetuating. In reality, Bank Leumi is too big, powerful, and unwieldy for the Jewish Agency to manage in an owner-chattel relationship. The Israeli government also deals with the bank at arm's length. In spite of a government rule that would permit the State Comptroller to inspect the bank's operations, the comptroller prefers to define the bank as a private enterprise.

Other Public Institutions

No survey on the margins of the Israeli state can overlook several public institutions that command substantial resources and do work of great prominence. Although they are legally distinct from the government, they are led by figures of importance in government circles. The universities have formed companies to develop land for industrial use and seek the commercial production of goods resulting from university laboratories. Companies of this kind fund research, arrange patent rights, and engage in joint ventures with multinational drug and medical supply firms.

The Jerusalem Foundation is a nonprofit association that is distinct from the municipality of Jerusalem. The foundation is the creation of Jerusalem's Mayor Teddy Kollek, who serves as its president and solicits most of the funds that come to it from related bodies in the United States, Canada, Great Britain, Germany, and South Africa. The Jerusalem Foundation is interesting because of the funds it channels to the mayor outside the framework of the public budget and government controls, amounting to about $7 million (U.S.) in 1976. Not only are the resources substantial in their own right but they gain importance when used as leverage to obtain government funds for projects begun with foundation money. The foundation gives the mayor some leverage over his nominal superior in the Interior Ministry.

The Jerusalem Foundation also supports projects that would run afoul of political alignments on the Municipal Council, such as pools for coeducational swimming or a sports stadium to be used on the Sabbath; both projects provoke opposition from religious parties. In terms of political theory, the foundation provides independence from governmental constraints to the mayor, who controls the foundation in his private capacity. Its list of projects include archeological excavations and restorations of historical sites, community centers and parks, maternal and child-care stations, subsidized theater tickets for schoolchildren, sports facilities, school buildings, neighborhood art studios, and religious institutions. Foundation personnel claim to move faster than municipal departments in obtaining clearances necessary for projects and getting physical structures in place.

The Jerusalem Foundation is not without its problems. It approaches prospective donors with a list of projects the mayor feels are

Figure 1. Ownership Structure: Israel Chemicals, Ltd., and its Subsidiaries

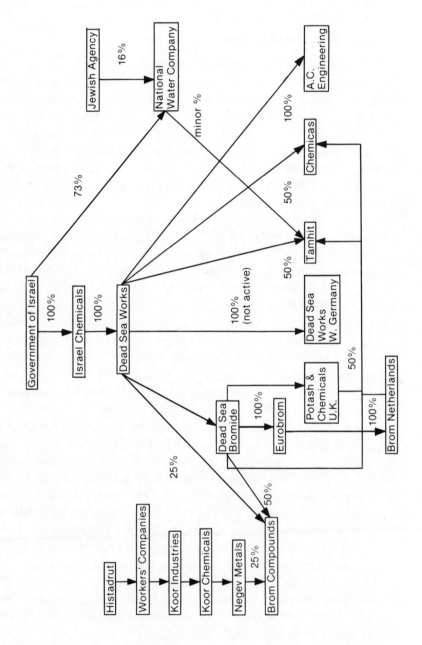

important, but some donors have strong ideas of their own. At times, foundation personnel have used their political credit with national ministries and departments of the municipality to obtain matching funds or construction permits for low-priority projects, justified solely on the basis of an important foreigner's passion to contribute. Critics charge that the mayor strengthens his political position with the foundation. He can trade a community center, park, or other facility for the cooperation of a neighborhood leader or a councilor on other matters. The mayors of Tel Aviv and Beersheba have sought to supplement their municipal resources with copies of the Jerusalem Foundation, but they cannot offer the setting and symbol of Jerusalem to potential donors.

Subsidiaries and Joint Ventures

Descriptions of companies owned by the State of Israel, the Labor Federation, the Jewish Agency, and other public bodies bring us only part of the way through the complexity on the margins of the Israeli state. Most companies on the margin are joint ventures between two or more public owners, or between them and private investors from Israel or abroad. There is no central record of companies in which the government owns some shares along with other investors and no central list of subsidiaries owned by companies that are themselves owned by the government, the Histadrut, or the Jewish Agency. There are also subsidiaries of subsidiaries ("second-generation" subsidiaries) as well as third- and fourth-generation subsidiaries. The tangle of ownership is complex, and raises questions about the chances for management control or political accountability. The tangle also multiplies the companies that can be cited for membership on the margins of the Israeli state. Curiosity alone would impel us to affix some number to the companies involved, their joint ventures, subsidiaries, and joint ventures among their subsidiaries; but no numbers are available. Figure 1 illustrates one pattern of ownership centered on Israel Chemicals, Ltd., gleaned from long hours of tracing shareholding in the Israeli Registry of Companies.

The organization begins simply enough. The government owns 100 percent of Israel Chemicals, which in turn owns 100 percent of Dead Sea Works. One level down, to the subsidiaries of Dead Sea Works and the subsidiaries of those subsidiaries, the picture becomes complex. Dead Sea Works has a 25 percent interest in Brom Compounds; another 25 percent in that same company is held by a third-generation subsidiary of Koor Industries, a unit of the Histadrut; and 50 percent of Brom Compounds is owned by a second-generation subsidiary of Dead Sea Works (i.e., Dead Sea Bromide). Dead Sea Bromide owns 100 percent of the shares in several companies established in Europe, and is partners with its own parent (Dead Sea Works) in two other firms. In one of these firms, a minor third partner is the National Water Company, which is itself owned partly by the government and partly by the Jewish Agency.

Jerusalem

A listing of important enterprises in Jerusalem illustrates the idiosyncratic development of services. Jerusalem's rail service is run by a government department. Household gas comes from competing firms, some of which are partly owned by government companies. The major provider of intraurban transport is a bus cooperative owned by its personnel, affiliated with the Histadrut, and dependent on the government for subsidies. Water comes from a municipal government department but is obtained from national water lines operated by a company 73 percent owned by the government, 16 percent owned by the Jewish Agency, and 11 percent owned by a variety of lesser partners. Health service comes primarily from an organ of the Histadrut but depends on the government for subsidies. Housing construction is divided among numerous corporations owned by the State of Israel, the Histadrut, the municipality, and private contractors; a department of the municipality regulates housing construction; and financing for housing comes through various mortgage banks owned by different public bodies. Social services come partly as a sideline of various public enterprises. Housing companies employ counselors and community organizers to work in neighborhoods they have built. Departments of the municipality, the Histadrut, the Jewish Agency, and national ministries offer their social services. And the Jerusalem Foundation helps the mayor fill in the gaps between programs of other providers. To help citizens sort their way through these various institutions, there are separate ombudsmen of the government, the municipality, the Jewish Agency, the Histadrut, and several national ministries.

GENERAL TRAITS ON THE MARGINS

The entrepreneurship of Israeli managers plus the existence of different public sectors lie behind the growth of parent companies, joint ventures, and subsidiaries. Each manager has an implicit license to hunt for resources. Ambitious managers prefer being directors of subsidiary firms rather than department heads within a larger body. If funds for a new venture are not available from the government Treasury, they may come from the profits of a government company looking for investment opportunities or from a company of the Histadrut or the Jewish Agency. The entrepreneurs of Israel's public sectors also travel the world looking for partners. They seek out Jewish and non-Jewish businessmen in North and South America, Europe, Australia, and South Africa. The new firm need not be incorporated in Israel or even have a dominant Israeli component in its management or product inputs. Indeed, within the tangle of firms with Israeli connections are some whose parentage is obscured deliberately. They facilitate commerce between Israel and countries that prefer not to acknowledge an Israeli connection.

The legal character of organizations on the margins of the Israeli state facilitates their wild multiplication. The typical organization is a limited-liability company organized under the general company law of Israel. This structure provides maximum flexibility for the government and other shareholders. The government can buy into a company to the extent of 1 percent or 100 percent of its shares. It can accept partners up to the percentage of shares not yet committed. An established company can issue additional shares in order to recruit more capital or more partners. Company law gives directors the option of establishing subsidiaries and joint ventures, and these develop to meet opportunities perceived by directors. The margins of the Australian state, in contrast, include few subsidiaries of the statutory authorities. The statutes of most Australian authorities do not provide for subsidiaries, and the typical Australian manager requires that his statute explicitly permit any action he contemplates.

It is simple to establish a parent company in Israel. For government-owned companies, the Economic Committee of Ministers can take the appropriate steps. No special enactment from the Knesset is needed. The motives for creating a new company, or spinning off a subsidiary, range across a wide spectrum from "public interest" to "pragmatic exploitation of a good opportunity."[7] Public interest justifications include the conventional reasons for the use of public resources: a project vital for reasons of economic development or political interest, but with a demand for capital or an element of risk beyond the means of private investors. Or there may be an implicit public interest in a project — say, power generation or vital transportation — that requires government control. In keeping with the national policy to promote immigration, some companies of the government, the Histadrut, and the Jewish Agency seek to provide employment as a primary goal, perhaps in a rural area that the government would like to settle. If such a firm can make something that was previously imported, then it will serve the secondary goal of saving foreign currency. Firms spring up as subsidiaries of public enterprise simply to take advantage of an opportunity that offers the prospect of commercial profit. Some enterprises have incorporated several subsidiaries that remain in reserve as empty shells. They can define a purpose and recruit staff when a member of the present management team spots an opportunity or when a private investor makes a proposal for a joint venture.

ENVIRONMENTAL INFLUENCES ON THE MARGINS

As is the case in Australia, no single factor influences the margins of the Israeli state in isolation from any other. Also as in Australia, elements of the political culture, the economy, and the structure of government have something to do with developments on the margins.

Political Culture

The political culture of Israel is predominantly Jewish. The entrepreneurialism observed in the companies of the government, the Labor Federation, and the Jewish Agency has been sharpened by millennia of wandering as a marginal people having to live by their wits. Jews serve as just about every sociologist's classic example of entrepreneurs. It would be surprising not to find this trait prominent in the public as well as the private sector of Israel. Some 85 percent of the population is Jewish. There is, to be sure, a heterogeneity in Israel born of recent migrations from one hundred countries of all continents; 48 percent of the Jewish population was born outside the country. Nevertheless, entrepreneurship is a trait that many immigrants nurtured in their previous homes and brought with them to Israel. Entrepreneurial behavior appears not only in publicly owned companies but also in the control units of government. It is up to government overseers of companies to make the best of their situation, both for their organizations and for themselves. A good job will add to an official's reputation and facilitate career advancement within the ministry or elsewhere.

The Israeli view of law reflects Israeli entrepreneurialism and also draws on religious roots. An essential feature of Judaism is the interpretation of law. Generations of talmudic exegesis have prepared Israeli managers to recognize not only what the law says but also what it does not say. Unlike the Australian manager, who feels inhibited unless the law explicitly permits an action, the Israeli manager feels comfortable as long as the law does not explicitly prohibit an action. Even then, he may search for conditions that will excuse him from a particular prohibition.

Entrepreneurialism is not the only feature that comes from the political culture to companies on the margins of the Israeli state. A heritage of different secular cultures has also made itself felt on Israel and its people. Israeli law and governmental procedure show the residue of the Ottoman Empire and the British Mandate, as well as three decades of Israeli enactments. The current generation of managers also reflects experiences from the countries that have provided Israel with its immigrants. Clashes between expectations and reality are inevitable in such a situation. Culture shock afflicts clients as well as company managers, who witness a continuing medley of strange encounters no matter how long they have lived in Israel.

One observer describes four principal cultures mixed together haphazardly in the public life of Israel:

1. A traditional Middle Eastern style, with a slow transaction of business, deference to authority, displays of officiousness, and an inclination toward bargaining with details of official decisions

2. A British legacy that appears in certain procedures, along with British predispositions to no-nonsense central control with little room for bargaining

3. Varied traditions brought by Jewish settlers from their countries of origin, which make for different cultures within the same workplace likely to breed misunderstandings and conflict

4. A self-styled Israeli approach identified with Zionist pioneers who were skilled in political in-fighting, confident in their inherent visionary powers, and committed to pragmatism, adaptability, and improvisation that verges on a lack of respect for rational planning[8]

Along with this variety of administrative cultures is a confusing medley of bureaucratic forms. Organizations have grown willy-nilly, with all the jumbled appearance of Middle Eastern cities whose lack of physical order frustrates efficient transportation. Like the traveler who must find directions through the streets of ancient Jerusalem, Acre, or Jaffa, the client or employee of Israel's bureaucracy is bound to encounter a convoluted route with unexpected turns and dead ends.

Also included in the political culture of Israel is a commitment to a full-service state. Widely available social services, extensive programs of education, and a commitment to full employment show obligations of charity from Judaism plus the nineteenth-century socialism that combined with the Zionist ideal of building a new society in Israel. Many Israelis feel that the socialist bloom has faded from their society, and hostile outsiders cite the country for heartlessness toward its poor. Both are wrong. Israel remains as much a socialist society as any, in terms of the proportion of resources controlled by public bodies or the extensiveness of social services. These commitments produce public involvement in every sector of the economy, with much of the involvement via corporations on the margins of the state.

The Economy

The principal influence on public companies that comes from the economy of Israel is the constant strain of insufficient resources. In per capita terms, Israel is among the wealthiest countries in the world. Yet there are not enough resources for the burdens imposed by inner aspirations and external constraints.

Israel's defense burden is enormous. In a recent year the budget of the Defense Ministry took 13 percent of gross national product, compared with equivalent figures of less than 3 percent for Australia and slightly more than 5 percent for the United States. Other costs for security weigh on the budgets of the Israeli police, El Al Airlines, and virtually all public institutions and commercial establishments that feel themselves vulnerable to terrorist attack. Economic boycotts organized by the Arab League have their impact on publicly owned companies in the guise of foregone opportunities. Each public body, as well as each private concern in the country, must add to its work force a factor of redundancy to cover for the thirty or more days each year (as recently as 1975 it was ninety days each year) that males serve in the military reserve.

There are personal as well as institutional signs of short resources. Salaries are lower on an international standard than is the cost of living, and workers often take second jobs. The result is reduced efficiency and increased tension in all organizations. Offices are spartan, crowded, and noisy; there is none of the plush carpet, rich paneling, or ample space of Australian executive suites. Phone lines are inadequate, entailing long delays and wrong connections. Typewriters are in such short supply that much of the paperwork is done by hand, with resulting problems of clarity and botched communication. Papers pile up on the floor and windowsills for lack of handy file cabinets, and eat further into the space. Not enough clerks or supervisors are well trained. Some work furiously, but perhaps inefficiently, next to others who gossip for lack of an assignment. A visit to a government office, bank, or insurance agency can be a harrowing experience. Desks may be cluttered with paper left over from previous visitors, and suggest the plight of one's own case. One can only hope that everything will get into the right file before it is stained with coffee or soup.[9] Clients rush to complete personal business in between their own jobs. Complex procedures and inadequate staffs produce frequent explosions of temper: between clients and staff or among the staff. Clients anticipate problems and scream even before it seems necessary. Israel's national ombudsman may receive the highest number of complaints per capita in the world.[10] In 1976, 400 complaints were submitted to the ombudsman against government mortgage banks and housing companies, and 190 were judged to warrant corrective action.[11] Economic constraints also affect the policies of government control units. It is government policy to minimize controls on joint ventures between government and private companies in order to encourage private investment, but businessmen continue to chafe under the controls that remain.

Structure of Government

The structure of government in Israel also has an influence on the margins of the state. By "government" here is meant the full range of institutions that allocate the public resources of Israel and have political mechanisms to select key officials and define major policies. In this concept of government, then, are not only the offices of the government but those of the Histadrut and the Jewish Agency.

This triumvirate of public sectors lies behind much of economic and social policy in Israel. Political science textbooks focus on the simple and centralized structure of the Knesset, government, and state bureaucracy, but this image hides more than it reveals. The structure is deceptively simple. There are no districts for the election of Knesset members; election is by proportional representation according to party lists from a single national constituency. The Prime Minister and his or her government are responsible to the Knesset, the bureaucracy is responsible to ministers of the government, and local authorities are subordinate to the Interior Ministry. Functions organized locally in the United States, such as police and education, are organized nationally in Israel.

The simple structure of the government becomes complex in its many contacts with the Histadrut and the Jewish Agency. Both institutions predate the government and are jealous of their separate status. For example, one of the political issues of the 1950s concerned the transfer of Histadrut schools to the Ministry of Education. And for several years there has been a struggle over the transfer of the Histadrut's Sick Fund to the Ministry of Health. With the Labor party out of the government for the first time in the State's history, the hold of the Histadrut on its Sick Fund seemed precarious. After a year and a half in office, however, the Likud government has not been able to nationalize health care.

One explanation for the continued trifurcation of Israeli public institutions is the preoccupation of national politics with international and defense policy. Almost all Prime Ministers have concentrated on international and military issues and have relegated domestic concerns — including the reorganization of domestic institutions — to lesser ministers and to their own back burner.

At several points it is necessary to look beneath the official structure of Israeli government to see what really happens. This is especially true in discussing municipalities. Formally they are subordinate to the national Interior Ministry with little autonomy of their own. Yet the mayors of Israel are as entrepreneurial as any company manager. Mayor Teddy Kollek of Jerusalem established fund-raising bodies in world capitals to provide money outside the framework of government controls. Mayor Shlomo Lahat of Tel Aviv presented the government with a fait accompli that forced unwanted decisions on the Interior Ministry. The mayor proceeded with urban renewal in spite of a negative decision from the ministry. By the time the ministry had processed the necessary injunctions through the court system, the mayor had a huge excavation in the middle of his city. On another occasion, Tel Aviv established a company along with partners from the private sector in order to create a huge bus station. The municipality and its partners raised only enough money to build the facility and not enough to clear surrounding land and connect the bus terminal with the road network. The station has been sitting as a white elephant, obviously waiting for the national government to tire of the eyesore and pay for the land, roads, and bridges needed to make it functional.

GOVERNANCE ON THE MARGINS

In Israel, as in Australia, we can generalize that managers of public enterprises have great independence. In the continuing tug of war between autonomy and accountability, autonomy usually wins. All the universal reasons favor autonomy, such as the need for managers able to cope with changing realities as they see fit, and the inability of central controllers to comprehend everything that could be placed under their jurisdiction. In Israel there are also lots of hard-driving entrepreneurs in the companies of the government, the Histadrut, and the Jewish Agency. They thrive on autonomy, and want to preserve it. Except when someone on the margins takes more advantage than is permitted by informal norms, most managers of public companies have a degree of independence that approaches that of private companies.

Although the scales weigh on the side of autonomy for Israeli managers, the people who argue for accountability also have accomplishments. They have built stronger institutions of government control than have their counterparts in Australia, for the entrepreneurial managers of Israel have invited more supervision. Routine controls on government companies come from personnel in the ministries. Additional supervision originates with the Authority for Government Companies and the State Comptroller. Both the Histadrut and the Jewish Agency have parallel activities with respect to their companies. By looking at organizations with no real equivalent in Australia, we can see both the efforts and the limitations of an activist approach to government control over the margins of the state.

Ministerial Control

Each government-owned company in Israel is assigned to a minister according to field of activity. As of 1976, the minister of finance had the most companies (39) under his jurisdiction, followed by the minister of commerce and industry (18), the minister of tourism (12), and the minister of housing (11). The principal linkages between ministers and companies are appointees to the companies' boards of directors—in number according to the proportion of a company's shares the government holds.

Government directors of major companies generally include senior civil servants in the ministry, whose government duties have something to do with the companies they help direct. In other words, key individuals have separate contacts with government companies: once as employees of a ministry that must pass on the company's request for funds or project approvals, and once as company directors who must deliberate about company plans including requests made to the ministry. The persons involved recognize the conflicts of interest. In one instance a person is a company advocate and a supplicant to the government; at another time, the same person acts for the government in response to the company's proposals. Benefits accrue to these controllers – and their ministerial superiors – in the form of information and understanding about the ministry's companies. There are also benefits for the company because there is a greater understanding of government policy. Officials admit to some concern about conflicting loyalties, but say that a company director's colleagues in the ministry should be able to spot excessive loyalties toward a company when they meet in ministerial committees that review company proposals. Decisions having major financial implications face separate reviews in the Finance Ministry. Also, the State Comptroller makes an independent review of major companies every few years. In the final analysis it is part of the government director's job to handle touchy issues of conflicting interest. Directors are, in fact, asked to serve in two related positions both for the benefit their expertise about government policy will bring to the company and for the benefit their expertise about the company will bring to the ministry.

Nongovernmental Public Companies

Each of the other principal owners of public companies in Israel – the Histadrut and the Jewish Agency – have adopted control procedures similar to those of the government. Committees from the policy-making organs must approve the establishment of a new company; directors appointed to the boards of the company are principal lines of communication between owner and company; and major decisions of each company have to clear special procedures in Histadrut or Jewish Agency bodies equivalent to the government's Finance Ministry. Both the Histadrut and the Jewish Agency have a company authority equivalent to the Government Companies Authority to maintain records and annual reports about each company's operations and finances. Also, both the Histadrut and the Jewish Agency have controllers who parallel the government's State Comptroller; they make periodic reviews of companies as well as other administrative entities of the Histadrut and the Jewish Agency.

The Problem of Joint Ventures

A problem arises when a company is a joint venture. *Who should review what is partly someone else's* seems to be a universal problem. It raises problems of delicate relations and limited resources. There is a reluctance to pry into someone else's terrain, especially when "someone else" is a national or international organization of importance and sensitive about its independence. There is also a limited amount of time and personnel that can be used to monitor companies, and so it is better to use them for monitoring companies that depend entirely on one's own resources. Such a strategy maximizes the control of companies that are clearly one's own and avoids territorial conflicts with bodies that co-own joint ventures. The result of this strategy is that joint ventures come in for less frequent and less incisive auditing than companies that are wholly or largely owned by the government, the Histadrut, or the Jewish Agency. No controller admits to overlooking something in his jurisdiction. With respect to joint ventures, officials at the core of all three public sectors claim to "keep our fingers on the pulse" of joint ventures, or assert that they take a close look when they "hear about problems." Similar issues appear in Australia and the United States. In both federal countries, control units of the national government are reluctant to probe how the states administer joint national-state programs. From their side, control units of state governments prefer to focus on programs financed by their government alone.

Authority for Government Companies

The Israeli Authority for Government Companies has impressive powers. It is located in the Finance Ministry, within chatting distance of the real muscle in domestic policy. The Government Companies Law of 1975 gives to the authority a set of formidable tools. In the words of the law, the authority shall

1. Advise the Government, through the Minister of Finance, and the Ministers (having substantive responsibility for the company) on matters relating to Government companies

2. In accordance with directives from the Government, deal with matters common to all Government companies or to particular classes thereof

3. Keep track of and assist in the implementation of the State Comptroller's recommendations relating to Government companies

4. Advise and assist Government companies in the conduct of their business

5. Keep constant track of the activities of each Government company, the implementation of its objects, the progress of its business, its financial position, its wage policy; and communicate its findings to the Ministers

6. Examine the reports submitted to it by a Government company and the material on which they are based and make its comments thereon to the company and the Ministers

7. Deal with and assist in the establishment, winding-up, and amalgamation of Government companies, as well as in compromise settlements and arrangements thereof and the restoration, reorganization and sale of shares thereof

8. Carry out, in respect of a Government company, any function entrusted to it by the Government or the Ministers

This statutory language is more suggestive than descriptive. It is not yet clear to what extent the authority will develop its potential. Its future activity will lie somewhere between that of a passive collator of information and an assertive competitor of the State Comptroller and substantive specialists in Finance and other ministries.

By early 1978 the authority had a staff of twelve people with training in economics for the general supervision of companies. Additional personnel survey wages and labor relations and check company directors with respect to conflicts of interests and attendance at board meetings. The staffing of the authority shows some promise of matching its legal potential. Like other central units in Israel and elsewhere, however, the authority seems to put most of its energy into the most visible parts of its jurisdiction (i.e., the companies owned wholly or largely by the government). During one interview, two of its senior officers could not agree whether the authority reviewed the appointment of government directors to the subsidiaries and joint ventures of government companies.

The authority has found some problems in its statutes. It is limited to the review of companies defined under the Government Companies

Law of 1975 (i.e., companies in which the government owns at least 50 percent of the stock or controls at least 50 percent of its direction). This means that the authority could avoid some companies like Zim Shipping where a minority government shareholdership (40 percent) is *more important* in terms of resources or control of vital infrastructure than a majority government shareholdership in numerous smaller and less sensitive companies. Like other Israeli organizations, the Authority for Government Companies does not let a narrow view of law stand in its way. Its annual report for 1976 included a synopsis on Zim plus twenty-eight other mixed companies and five that it described as "without standing under the Government Companies Law."[12]

The State Comptroller

The Israeli State Comptroller deserves special attention. The comptroller is the auditor of government activities, accountable to the Knesset. The office is, by design, independent of the government so that work can be done unhindered by partisan or institutional loyalties. Israel's State Comptroller has equivalents in most democracies. For our concern with the accountability of units on the margins of the state, the auditor may be critical. The issue is not so much the legal authority that lies at his discretion, or at the discretion of the legislature to which he reports. That authority is likely to be considerable. More important is the question of how well equipped the auditor is to find out what is really happening at the margins of the state. *What kind of a staff does the State Comptroller have? What questions are the staff trained to ask? How dogged are they in following the scent of problems to their source?*

There are considerable differences between Israel's State Comptroller and Australia's Auditors General (at Commonwealth and state levels).[13] The Israeli State Comptroller has more skilled investigators, and they ask more incisive questions. While Australia's Auditors General tend to stop with a concern for proper financial records, the Israeli State Comptroller is concerned with the effectiveness and efficiency of the programs. The comptroller tackles questions of great complexity and is willing to challenge experts in the ministries and government companies. Yet the State Comptroller also has limitations. Units on the margins of the Israeli state retain considerable operating autonomy, in spite of the comptroller's inquiries. By looking at both the resources and the limitations of this auditing body we can come to an understanding of some factors that work to keep marginal units on the margins of governmental concern even in the presence of well-equipped and aggressive government control.

To understand the activities of Israel's State Comptroller it is helpful to look at the range of activities undertaken by its counterparts in other countries. The simple label of "state auditor" does not convey much information about the functions and powers of an office. Looking at comparable institutions in various countries, it is possible to find different approaches with respect to topics audited, the character of audits undertaken, and the uses of audit findings. State auditors can

Audit government companies themselves or rely on the work of audit firms in the private sector that apply the same procedures to government companies as to private firms

Focus audit activities on the financial recordkeeping of government companies or review the merits of general policies and specific projects

Limit sanctions to the report of audit findings or, depending on legal capacity, exercise such prerogatives as stopping the flow of government financing for projects judged to be improper

Audit all entities in which the government has a stake or confine audits to certain classes of entities

The law that defines the jurisdiction of Israel's State Comptroller is generous by international standards. The State Comptroller's office can audit any company in whose direction the government has a share; it is not limited to companies in which the government share of direction is at least 50 percent, as is the case with the Government Companies Authority. Subsidiaries of government companies cannot be audited without a specific decision by the State Comptroller, or by the Knesset committee that reviews the comptroller's activities. Moreover, the State Comptroller does not audit second- or higher-generation subsidiaries (subsidiaries of subsidiaries, subsidiaries of subsidiaries of subsidiaries, and so on) or any subsidiaries outside Israel that are not completely Israeli owned.

The State Comptroller faces an open-ended statutory invitation with respect to criteria used in auditing corporations. Aside from conventional checks on financial recordkeeping and the legality of corporate revenues and expenditures, the comptroller may determine "whether the inspected bodies have operated economically, efficiently and in a morally irreproachable manner."

The sanctions available to the State Comptroller are more limited than the jurisdiction. The State Comptroller can report findings publicly, to responsible authorities in the corporations audited, to the Finance Ministry, to the Knesset, and in the case of suspected criminal violations, to the Justice Ministry. In this the State Comptroller resembles most counterparts elsewhere; it does not have operative sanctions. The office does not have the power of the U.S. Comptroller General to stop payments for activities carried on contrary to law.

The State Comptroller's administrative resources are impressive, but are not so great as to constitute a commanding position over the audited companies. Forty professionals, divided among four units of the State Comptroller, concentrate on government companies. The personnel of other units deal with companies as part of their inquiries into the ministries in charge of them. Most persons who concentrate on government companies are graduates in economics or business administration, or are certified public accountants. They may call on in-house specialists in economics, law, engineering, agriculture, and shipping. On occasions when a case requires unusual expertise or immediate attention, the State Comptroller contracts audits to professionals outside the organization.

The staff of the State Comptroller has routine procedures for planning activities. Criteria for selecting audit targets include the date of the last audit, with most companies audited every five or ten years, depending on the size of the company's capital or turnover; current public interest in the company (defined by statements in the Knesset, articles in media, or communications with the State Comptroller); the character of information accumulating in the files of the State Comptroller about each company; and the availability of appropriate personnel to do the audit. Some of the largest firms, like El Al Airlines and Israel Aviation Industry, receive continuous attention by State Comptroller personnel.

Ranking officials report that units dealing with government companies carry high prestige within the State Comptroller organization and command many of the "best people" for their staffs. Other high-ranking audit units deal with big spenders and prominent ministries like Defense and Finance. As in other bureaucracies, however, the State Comptroller's units for government companies must also take their share of dead wood. Planners admit that they allocate more than average attention to small and unproblematic companies because certain tenured auditors can only handle such assignments.

The subsidiaries of government companies receive separate treatment in the State Comptroller's plans. Their large number and separate status in the law (requiring a special decision to audit by the State Comptroller or the Knesset committee) produce a presumption against auditing them. In order to break through this presumption, a subsidiary must score in a distinctive manner on one or several planning criteria. That is, its investment or turnover must be particularly high, there must be considerable public interest, or information in the State Comptroller's files must suggest serious problems. This presumption of special need exists in more heightened form for a branch office or a subsidiary located outside Israel. In this case, the need to spend foreign exchange for the audit is an extra constraint that works against control. It is even less likely that the State Comptroller will audit second-generation subsidiaries (i.e., subsidiaries of subsidiaries). In what appears to be a narrow interpretation, the comptroller's staff read their law as excluding these bodies from their responsibility.

Special considerations also figure in audits of joint ventures. For some of these, the State Comptroller will alternate audits and share information in a systematic fashion with counterpart audit units in the Histadrut or the Jewish Agency. With many of the joint ventures, the inclination is to leave audit responsibilities elsewhere. These companies have a great deal of freedom from state monitoring, at least until a problem stirs the Knesset to make a special request, or stirs the State Comptroller's office to employ its jurisdiction over bodies in which the state has some share.

Findings and Reports of the State Comptroller

It is not easy to characterize the audit findings of the State Comptroller about government companes. One study done by a former staff member, and published by the comptroller, emphasizes the organization's concentration on matters of procedure: whether company executives follow established rules for consulting with boards of directors and ministerial superiors; whether the companies insist on their full rights in transactions with private partners, and whether the appropriate reports are filed on time. From this perspective, the State Comptroller follows a safe course, avoiding details of program design that auditors (many of whom are accountants) are not trained to assess.[14]

Some personnel of the State Comptroller challenge this view. They point to difficult issues their colleagues have tackled, such as decisions of Israel Aviation Industry to invest in the design and production of major civilian and military projects.

There may be a point of balance between these opposing views. On the one side, there are cases when the State Comptroller takes on difficult issues requiring technical expertise and close judgment. On the other side, a great deal of what the comptroller does with respect to government companies is to cite faults in routine procedures of management.

Critics of the State Comptroller fear that it will induce corporations to protect themselves by an excessive concern with internal procedures at the expense of appropriate risks. In the context of the Israelis' habit of burdening themselves with too many clerks and a surplus of paperwork, it is unfortunate that the State Comptroller has not given more attention to these obvious problems of public corporations. Indeed, the State Comptroller may be exacerbating the problem of excessive red tape with its focus on proper procedure.

The State Comptroller makes its own considerable contribution to the paper that circulates among government offices in Israel. Its annual report, which summarizes numerous reports published during the year about government departments and companies, runs to 1200 pages. Additional reports—perhaps 20 a year, each running 50-120 pages—detail findings about individual firms. A yearly volume of comments by the Finance Ministry in response to the State Comptroller's annual report is about 500 pages long; three shorter volumes of the Finance Ministry deal with the recommendations of a ministerial committee in response to the comptroller's reports, and with the repair of defects cited by the comptroller. Other volumes come from the Knesset committee that reviews State Comptroller reports. On occasion the State Comptroller has published, in English as well as Hebrew, *Selected Findings on Matters of Principle* and *Norms for Public Administration* based on several years' reports about government corporations and other public bodies.[15] Another summary volume, as well as annual reports, deals with the State Comptroller's other role, that of ombudsman.

The State Comptroller has also contributed to the international literature about state control. In 1973 it published Joseph Douer's *State Audit of Government Corporations in Israel: Characteristic Findings, Shortcomings in Matters of Principle and Their Treatment by State*

Organs in the Years 1960-1970. In 1976 members of the comptroller's staff prepared a series of papers on the control of government corporations for a seminar sponsored jointly by the United Nations, the International Organization of Supreme Audit Institutions, and the German Foundation for International Development. Both the Douer volume and the collections of papers compare favorably with literature produced by audit units of major countries and with anthologies on the administration of government corporations produced by the UN Department of Economic and Social Affairs.[16]

Analyses and reports prepared by Israel's State Comptroller rate high by international standards. Nevertheless, there is a good chance that the managers of public corporations will escape effective supervision and sanction because of a shortage of systematic follow-up to the State Comptroller's detailed reports. Routine procedures exist for following up reports on government departments, typically two years after the original citation of a problem. But follow-up activities must compete with new audits for audit personnel within the State Comptroller's organization. Only a few citations of difficulties actually receive a formal review. *As a matter of policy, reports on government companies receive no formal follow-up.* In discussing these arrangements, personnel assert that follow-up is informal and continuous. They report that working auditors and their unit heads stay on top of the reports that come routinely from government companies, as well as extralegal transmissions that come from the mass media plus bureaucratic friends and neighbors. According to these claims, several fingers are always on a company's pulse. Moreover, auditors seek to keep company managers honest by requesting informally about the repair of defects cited in earlier reports. The ultimate weapon of the auditor is the next full-scale audit, as a result of which a company manager may find himself criticized in the media, the Knesset, and a ministry for past shortcomings not corrected, as well as for any new shortcomings.

It is difficult to evaluate claims of being on top of companies between formal audits and assertions about informal contacts between auditors and companies. Undoubtedly some auditors can screen large amounts of information in a way that tells them when things are amiss in certain firms. Nevertheless, serious problems are involved in such pulse-feeling at the same time that other companies are being audited actively and each day's paperwork is being prepared. There is a component of accident or randomness in an auditor's realization that something is amiss in a company substantially before the problem arouses the mass media.

The ultimate limit of the State Comptroller's effectiveness is its dependence on persuasion. Like most other state auditors, the office lacks definite powers to stop the activities of government companies, or other bodies, that it considers improper or unwise. One sign of this dependence on persuasion is the introspective character of senior officials. Officials discuss *honest differences of opinion* between the State Comptroller and audited bodies as well as *not-so-honest differences of opinion*. An honest difference of opinion occurs when the State Comptroller makes a point of criticism while conceding within its organization that the case has some weakness. When the target of the criticism makes a sharp defense against the criticism, there is a sense of fair dispute, which the State Comptroller can lose gracefully. A dishonest difference of opinion occurs when the targets of criticism invent spurious reasons to excuse culpability. In these instances the State Comptroller is less inclined to make a moderate defense of its position and pursues the matter by orchestrating information for the media and the Knesset. It is not surprising that the State Comptroller prefers cases that are clear and of likely interest to the public and politicians. For an organization dependent on persuasion, blacks and whites are better than shades of gray. In gray areas, after all, there may be no controls capable of overcoming specialists in government companies.

The Israel Coins and Medals Corporation presented an ideal target for the State Comptroller. It deals in simple, tangible items: commemorative medals and coins sold to collectors of numismatic artifacts. In many respects its record is admirable. Its products bring escalating prices in the world market and an annual profit to the company and the Israeli Treasury. Nonetheless, the company's managers engaged in activities that were obviously improper. They gave or sold medals and coins below market value to favored employees, directors, members of the Knesset, and certain others. Because the corporation's coins and medals multiply in value several times over, these free or below-cost distributions brought real wealth to the people chosen by the company's managers. They also made tangible demonstrations of corporate wrongdoing. The State Comptroller's report on the company received prominent coverage in the media.[17]

More difficult for the State Comptroller was the massive Israel Aviation Industry. It has a work force of almost 16,000 and an annual income of over a billion Israeli pounds, compared with the 60 workers and one hundred million pounds of the medals and coins company. In spite of these gross differences in scale, the State Comptroller's report on the Aviation Industry was barely twice the length of its report on the medals and coins company (117 versus 58 pages). The report on the Aviation Industry did tackle some difficult issues of technical judgment. But the report moved from topic to topic, and emphasized descriptive reportage over cogent summary or recommendations. The reader was left without guidance as to which of the alleged problems of the company were serious, or which should be the target of corrective measures.[18]

At times the State Comptroller has failed to reckon with compelling evidence in its own files. The State Comptroller also takes on the role of national ombudsman of Israel. Its reports have shown one government company — Amidar: The National Company to House Immigrants in Israel — ranking with the telephone service and the Education Ministry as attracting the largest number of citizen complaints. Yet there is no detailed analysis of these complaints to the ombudsman in the most recent audit report on Amidar by the State Comptroller. That audit cites various problems of the company, but with no systematic effort to identify the most central of the company's faults, or to make precise recommendations for change that could be checked by a subsequent audit.[19]

All told, there seems to be a random component to the State Comptroller's review of government companies. Chances are that a particular issue will not attract the attention of its staff or achieve prominence in its reports. Even if an issue does surface, subsequent audits are likely to avoid any systematic follow-up. The managers of Israel's government companies see a myriad of controllers in ministerial employees, the Authority for Government Companies, and the State Comptroller. They also recognize many cracks in the network of control. Aggressive managers spend some of their time calculating the chances of getting caught while taking a procedural short-cut.

Any analysis directed at reforming the control of companies on the margins of the Israeli state should recognize subtle advantages in the status quo. While the likelihood of an Israeli government company having to account for particular decisions is subject to chance, the unknown factor in accountability has some worth. Company officials are more fearful of an audit than they otherwise might be. Fear may help keep their behavior within acceptable bounds. Such a situation may be no less desirable than a sharply increased audit coverage, especially if increased auditing emphasizes the use of conventional paperwork for planning and reporting. The optimum situation would be just the right amount of audit coverage, with auditors who balance a concern for enough corporate procedures with a concern for too much red tape. Yet these are elusive standards, especially for countries like Israel, which have shortages of well-trained and sensitive administrators.

SOME COSTS AND BENEFITS
ON THE MARGINS

The incoherence that prevails on the margins of the Israeli state poses obvious problems of management and political accountability. There are duplications, overlapping responsibilities, confusion among clients and policy makers as to what government company is suited to what activity, and a great number of justified complaints to the ombudsman.

The housing field alone provides cogent illustrations of incoherence on the margins. The government, the Histadrut, the Jewish Agency, and several municipalities have companies that construct residential housing as well as grant mortgage loans. Some firms have particular missions, such as providing housing or loans to immigrants, young couples, or large families. Yet the differences among the companies are not always clear, and company procedures can be complex to the point of self-destruction. For example, one government housing company refused to quote a final price for an apartment before the customer signed a purchase contract. The government mortgage bank, however, would not commit itself to a loan until it received a firm price from the housing company. Each party had a point. The housing company did not want to quote a price in an escalating market (30 to 40 percent annual inflation) when the mortgage bank might delay its approval — and the housing company's receipt of its money — by several months; and the mortgage bank did not want to start its procedures without a firm price being set for the apartment. Each of the government companies was looking after itself; both were ignoring the client. Moreover, with all the mortgage banks of the three public sectors plus numerous private institutions, no banks are prepared to give mortgages that begin to cover the price of an apartment. It is common for a couple to assemble a down payment of 50 percent of the purchase price from a combination of personal savings and family collections and then amass the remainder through five or six mortgages and loans from different public and private banks. The whole process is likely to take several months of intense labor. Numerous purchases flounder with the collapse of delicately stacked finance plans. It is little wonder that the government ombudsman recorded four hundred complaints against government housing companies and mortgage banks in 1976 and saw many of the complaints as justifiable.

With all these problems, the multiplicity of publicly owned companies and entrepreneurial managers adds important flexibility to a beleaguered state. For one thing, a host of companies attached to one or another public sector helps in the accumulation of significant financial resources outside the tax network. Israel's tax burden is among the highest in the world, largely because of defense obligations. Companies of the government, the Histadrut, and the Jewish Agency carry much of the burden of developing an infrastructure and providing social services outside the tax framework — partly through reinvested profits and partly through capital raised in Israel and abroad as loans, investments, and gifts.

Publicly owned companies also offer program flexibility. Ministers can ask heads of companies to take on a project that does not fit within the resources or the competence of ministry employees. Sometimes the project may be risky politically and should be handled by an organization that is nominally autonomous. For example, a politician might ask a company or the Histadrut to absorb deserving party members who need employment. Or a development town populated by restive immigrants may be targeted for a new plant capable of absorbing unemployed youth, with a community center and counseling set up by the Jewish Agency.

Publicly owned companies and other bodies on the margins of the state offer special advantages in dealing with some of the sticky issues that abound in Israel. A combination of the Government Company to Redevelop the Jewish Quarter of the Old City and the Jerusalem Foundation has made a start on one issue in the Old City of Jerusalem. The issue concerns television antennas, which sprout like unsightly whiskers on otherwise picturesque stone and earth roofs. The municipality and the government would like to replace the individual antennas with a community antenna and cable connections to individual homes. But there are two problems. The first is anticipated hostility from Arab residents of the Old City, who would cite the project as one more effort by the Jewish administration to impose permanence on its occupation of the Old City. The second is anticipated demands from Jewish and non-Jewish residents outside the Old City. If the government or the municipality subsidized a community television antenna and cables for residents of the Old City, why not also for residents of the New City? A combination of a government company and a private foundation can handle both these problems. They can target special projects without obliging a government department to provide services equally to all members of the population. Thus the Jerusalem Foundation has provided the money and the Government Company to Redevelop the Jewish Quarter of the Old City has provided program administration. The work started in the Jewish and Armenian quarters, viewed as the most receptive politically. Next in line is the Christian Quarter. By the time the work progresses to the Moslem Quarter, likely to be the most suspicious, it is hoped that residents will have heard from the Armenian and Christian quarters about the improved television reception available without financial outlay or physical damage to homes.

Problems over the new sports stadium also led the Jerusalem municipality to rely on the margins of the state. The problems here reflect three aspects of the city: one large group of the population observes Saturday afternoon football rituals to the point of fanaticism; another large component is devoutly religious and views desecration of the Sabbath in the most serious terms; and there is a shortage of land suitable for a sports stadium. No department of the government would involve itself in building a sports stadium that would lead to desecration of the Sabbath in Jerusalem—especially when the most suitable plot of vacant land abuts a religious neighborhood! Devout Jews have gone to great lengths in defending their views of proper behavior. They have pulled their members from delicately balanced coalitions at the municipal and national levels. Residents of religious neighborhoods have blocked major traffic arteries on the Sabbath to force the police to close the roads officially. They have stoned cars that have driven through their neighborhoods on the Sabbath and have destroyed a public swimming pool built in spite of their protests.

The issue of the sports stadium is still unresolved. It has been shunted to the margins of the state and, it is hoped, to the fringes of public awareness. The Jerusalem Foundation is providing much of the money. The administrative vehicle is a corporation owned by the foundation along with the municipality of Jerusalem, the National Sports Authority, and a sports association.

In spite of their many benefits, the units on the margins of Israel can offer too much of a good thing. Not far away from the exploitation of opportunity for public benefit is the exploitation of opportunity for private benefit. There may be no more than a thin line between an entrepreneur and a thief. Israel has its share of the world's scoundrels, and some of them operate in government companies and other autonomous units. Small and large scandals have taken place on the margins of the Israeli state.

One of the small scandals occurred within the Israel Coins and Medals Corporation when the company officers were distributing commemorative coins and medals to personal friends and business associates. This, as noted earlier, was uncovered by the State Comptroller.

Higher on the scale of peculation is the case of Asher Yadlin. His activities as chief executive of the Histadrut's Sick Fund included the receipt of bribes and kickbacks from construction contractors and improper use of Sick Fund money to purchase a hospital project begun by a group of Latin-American physician-investors. The case titillated the Israeli public for much of 1977, and it drags on through appeals and new allegations. The story broke when Yadlin — long an up-and-coming stalwart of the Labor party — was tapped by then Prime Minister Yitzhak Rabin as governor-designate of the Bank of Israel just at the point when the Israel police (unknown to the Prime Minister) were reaching the advanced stages of a criminal investigation. As Yadlin's appointment was being formally considered by the government, he was jailed for questioning. The case featured a loyal wife and a girl friend plus a business associate and party colleague of Yadlin who faced jail rather than testify against him. It roused old squabbles within the Labor party: Whose man was Yadlin? How could Rabin have announced his appointment while a formal investigation was under way? Yadlin, who may have channeled some illegal payments to the Labor party's treasury, claimed that he faced jail for doing what previous party leaders had accepted as common practice — using opportunities afforded by organizations on the margins of the state (in this case, the Histadrut) to accumulate funds for the ruling party.

MANAGERIAL CONTROL AND
POLITICAL ACCOUNTABILITY

Both management and political accountability suffer under the unfettered individualism and countless public enterprises on the margins of the Israeli state. Incoherence multiplies even though good work gets done under difficult circumstances. The Israeli problem is partly the confluence of different public sectors. Being at the heart of world Jewry has problems as well as benefits for Israel. The rich aunts and uncles of the diaspora make demands for distinctive programs, demands tailored to their own ideas. Within the Israeli community, the Histadrut will not submerge its institutions into those of the government. Now that the Labor party is outside the government, but still controls the Histadrut, there is a political factor working for distinctive Histadrut policies even while it is linked with government companies in uncounted joint ventures.

Finally we have the issue of Israeli entrepreneurialism. The essence of an entrepreneur is independence. The public-sector entrepreneur offers the great assets of creativity and hard work, but the same person causes problems for tight management and political accountability. Israel deals with entrepreneurs on the margins of the state by relying on the entrepreneurial behavior of control agents in Finance and other ministries, as well as in the State Comptroller's organization. The use of entrepreneurialism against itself has aesthetic appeal. It offers promise as an innovative approach to management, as well as assuring excitement for political scientists attracted to the Israeli arena of struggle between the margins and the core of a modern state.

4

THE UNITED STATES: SPECIAL AUTHORITIES AND GOVERNMENT CONTRACTORS

Americans love the process of government. They have created some 21,500 general-purpose governments (states, counties, municipalities), each with the power to collect revenue and design public services. They elect 521,758 officeholders ranging from the profound (e.g., the President) to the ridiculous (e.g., wharf masters and fence inspectors). Governments in the United States employ more people than the total populations of most countries of the world. The 18 million employees of American governments surpass the combined populations of Australia and Israel.

While the *governments* of the United States are big, units on the margins of the American state may be even bigger. Unfortunately there are no handy figures — either by the number of people employed or amount of money spent — to indicate the total size of governments plus quasi-governmental units.

It is no easy task to estimate what is and is not included in major reports about government employees and spending. The most prominent reports hide as much information as they reveal. The number of federal government employees shows only a modest growth from 1955 to 1976, and an 8 percent *decline* in employees relative to general population. Over the same period there were great expansions in social services; new government regulations covering industrial safety and air and water quality; and other programs in housing, energy, and mass transportation. Federal expenditures per capita increased by 157 percent, even controlling for inflation. How to explain the gap between a decline in personnel and in increase in expenditures? Some of the explanation appears in the growth of state and local governments; their growth came partly through money from Washington. State and local work forces increased by 141 percent over the 1955-76 period. But some of this growth was paid for by increased state and local revenues, apart from federal aid. Revenues increased by over 400 percent in real terms, again accounting for inflation. There is something missing in the records of the federal government. It is doing more now than in 1955 — even more than is accounted for by increased aid to state and local governments. Could it be that the efficiency of federal workers is improving? Could slightly more workers be accounting for a great deal more spending and all the programs enacted by the Johnson, Nixon, Ford, and Carter administrations? It seems improbable. The efficiency of clerical, administrative, and service workers — which is what constitutes much of the federal work force — does not increase rapidly.

The answer is that other workers employed by the federal government are not counted as government employees per se. They work for uncounted business firms, foundations, universities, and other organizations that do work for the government on a contract basis. Only scattered reports document this component of federal activity. Congress has insisted on data showing how much the Defense Department spends, by state, on primary contractors. Figures for 1975 showed Connecticut leading on a population basis, with $763 per capita of defense contracts. California led in the absolute magnitude of contracts, with $7.9 billion. This information is meant to appease congressional appetites for showing good work in behalf of industries back home. Even these records are incomplete, however. Most sizable contracts for military equipment are divided into many parts. A primary contractor for aircraft, for example, may parcel out one subcontract for the wings, another for the engines, a third for electronic gear, and so on. No published record accounts for the distribution of these secondary contracts across the country.

Outside the military sphere, only occasional tidbits — many of them unofficial — gauge the government work done by contractors. One source claims that about one third of the federal budget for various goods and services goes to contractors.[1] Another source puts the employees of contractors to the U.S. Department of Health, Education, and Welfare at 750,000, compared with 157,000 who work directly for the department. In 1976, 80,000 federal employees worked to oversee the administration of contracting.[2] The Department of Defense arranged some 10.4 *million* contracts in one year, for a total $46 billion.[3] The latest catalog of government contractors seems to have been assembled in 1948 — by a contractor. More recently, contractors have conducted courses for federal employees on how to arrange and supervise contracts.[4]

Yet another activity on the margins of the American state involves special authorities. These, too, defy enumeration. The most complete recent study estimates that these authorities spend more money for capital projects (buildings, facilities, major equipment) than all state and municipal governments combined.[5]

Both the number and variety of bodies on the margins of the American state are mind-boggling. They are consistent with the cacophony of government that can be found amid the 56 departments and "major" independent agencies of the national government, the 50 states, 3044 counties, and 18,517 municipalities.

WHY CREATE SPECIAL AUTHORITIES?

Numerous special authorities with business activities ranging from airports to zoos appear on the margins of the American state. It may be easiest to learn the overt function by the authority's title: a Turnpike Authority builds and maintains roads; a Water and Sewer District connects homes and businesses to its reservoirs, wells, and sewerage treatment; a Library Board runs the public library and its branches. In each special authority, however, several functions may be latent, secondary, or hidden. These include tasks to raise revenue outside the framework of the state or municipal budget and thereby avoid state constitutional or legal restrictions — or political pressures — against tax rates or indebtedness. Some authorities borrow against the income expected from the facilities they are about to construct, such as toll roads, college dormitories, or hospitals. Others borrow in order to build industrial sites for private industry and thereby tie loans to the authority's good fortune in finding tenants who will pay rent over the long haul. Pennsylvania is a heavy user of authorities that borrow money in order to build schools for lease to local communities. New York pioneered "moral obligation" bonds. The state legislature made a commitment to stand behind these bonds, but the commitment was *explicitly not a legal obligation.*

Another latent function of special authorities is to serve the multiple jurisdictions of a metropolitan area. It is impossible in most cases to persuade the central city and its suburbs to merge into a unified local authority, but it is possible to create area-wide police forces, library districts, airport authorities, and water-sewer districts.

Some special authorities also serve as an outlet for the ambitions of their executives. In the last chapter I reported on Israeli entrepreneurialism with its roots in Jewish history. American entrepreneurs hark back to the Yankee trader. For entrepreneurs, the special authority has the appeal of autonomy. Special authorities are usually on the margins of executive and legislative awareness, protected by statutory language that prohibits involvement by government officials in day-to-day management. Authorities that borrow for capital projects can be tied more closely to a consortium of bankers and insurance companies than to the government. There is a close fit between the swashbuckling image that the heads of some authorities have purveyed and the antigovernment sentiments that appear prominently in American culture. Thus, the head of an authority established by government, operating on funds obtained through commitments made or implied by governments, can obtain practical independence with the help of rhetorical forays against "political interference."

WHY CONTRACT?

Government contracts also serve manifest and latent functions. Manifest functions range from the pedestrian to the profound:

Janitorial and security service for government buildings

Cafeteria service for government employees

Design, construction, installation, operation, and/or service of equipment, facilities, and supplies (ranging from paper clips to office buildings, rifles to ICBMs)

Problem analysis and definition (i.e., to determine just what is wrong and what government may do to fix it)

Program design (drafting legislation, writing administrative manuals)

Program delivery (e.g., operating health clinics, halfway houses, counseling services, job training, etc.)

Selecting personnel to manage or work in government departments

Program monitoring and evaluation (i.e., determining what a government agency — or another contractor — is doing, and whether it is doing a good job)

In short, officers contract out virtually any work that the government could do with its own personnel. An exception is the actual approval of public policy. This is reserved, constitutionally, to members of the executive, legislative, and judicial branches. Nevertheless, the President, members of Congress, and justices of the Supreme Court — or their equivalents in state governments — do contract for information and advice, with an eye to the decisions they will make.

In order to identify the *latent functions* of contracting, it is necessary to follow our sensitive noses. The key question is this: Why should government contract out what it may otherwise do in-house? Answers include

To abide by requirements to freeze the size of the civil service even while adding to or enlarging the programs being offered

To purchase services cheaper than they can be had using government employees (contractors may pay lower wages, and may avoid the fringe benefits required for government employees)

To weaken the power of government employees' unions by giving work to contractors

To evade civil service regulations of various sorts (e.g., veterans' preference, maximum salary rules, a prohibition against paying moving expenses to new employees, or affirmative action procedures) by contracting out a project (the contractor is responsible for staffing, and may be limited only by a total amount that can be spent on "personnel")

To reward certain persons for favors rendered in the past by giving them a contract

To provide certain programs on a one-time or one-project basis, or experimentally, without risking continuation beyond a certain date that can be fixed in a contract

To save money on the cost of building (government may avoid the need to pay the entire cost of a building at the time of its construction by contracting for its rent over an extended period of time; the contractor will build the building and borrow for its construction, then include an amount for mortgage payments in the annual rental fee charged to government)

WHO ARE THE CONTRACTORS?

The population of government contractors is large and diverse. The field of research and development for military and space features major corporations that have long been known as contractors with the government: Lockheed, Boeing, and Litton, to name a few. Other profit-making companies have reputations in the area of designing administrative systems or doing program evaluation: Arthur D. Little, for example, or Peat, Marwick, Mitchell and Company. Some contractors are units of major companies, spun off from those activities popularly associated with the corporate name; for example, firms like Westinghouse and Greyhound operate cafeterias and do maintenance in government buildings. Numerous departments and institutes associated with universities contract with government agencies to provide research. Prominent among the users of these services are the National Science Foundation, National Institutes of Health, Office of Education, and the departments of Defense, Agriculture, Justice, and Housing and Urban Development.

There are lots of small fry among contractors. A local family business may win a city contract for trash pickup. A moonlighting professor of public administration may give a training program for managers of government programs. A graduate student may see an opportunity for profit in a paper written for a political science seminar. He can form a company and offer to pursue federal aids for local authorities, with payment contingent on success in finding money.

Some agencies widely viewed as charities have emerged as important contractors in the delivery of social services. Agencies linked with United Fund campaigns and those sponsored by the major religious denominations have come to receive more money from government contracts than from their traditional fund drives. As contractors they operate sheltered workshops for the handicapped, counsel clients in need of job training or medical services, arrange for vocational rehabilitation, and operate halfway houses for mental patients or criminal offenders. Many of these agencies carry the label of long-established church welfare societies, but they have opened their services to all clients as a condition for receiving government money.

One study of government payments to Jewish-sponsored social service agencies shows an increase from $27 million to $561 million over the 1962-73 period. Government payments went from 11 to 51 percent of the total income received by Jewish-sponsored agencies. Another study, of United Way agencies in the San Francisco area, found a doubling in the purchase of certain social services over the 1970-75 period.[6] Of the $145 million that New York City spent on day care, homemaker service, and foster care in 1969, $108 million (75 percent) went to voluntary organizations. In 1968 Pennsylvania allocated 88 percent of its spending for certain child-care programs to voluntary agencies.[7]

In treating government contractors as one class of creatures on the margins of the American state, this book departs from convention. It is more common to write about discrete classes of contracting: research and development, management consultants, service providers, or not-for-profit bodies. But this compartmentalization overlooks the common features of contracting that are the subject of this chapter. Indeed, my principal concern is to show the commonalities that government contractors of different kinds share with special authorities in the United States, as well as with the government companies of Israel and the statutory authorities of Australia.

COMMOTIONS ON THE MARGINS

Neither the development of special authorities nor contracting proceeds quietly; both have warm supporters and intense opponents. There are stories of beautiful successes and horrible failures, each mingled with simple ideology, myth, and personal stakes. Among the supporters of special authorities and contracting are right-wing reformers who react negatively to symbols of government and politics. They pride the creativity, hard work, and efficiency of the private sector. As Representative Jack Kemp (R-NY) wrote in a pro-contracting statement to a U.S. House of Representatives committee inquiry:

I do not believe government has any business being in business. I see no reason why it should compete with the private sector in providing goods and service.... A dollar spent in-house by government simply does not buy the same level of productivity as one spent in the private sector.... Competition has lost. Govern-

ment is forcing itself into obtaining more and more of its goods and services without the benefit of competition....America's technological lead is lost. In large measure this is because of the way in which increasing percentages of the innovative, creative processes associated with research and development are being moved into the too often stale environments of the bureaucracies.[8]

It has been government policy since 1967 to "rely upon the private enterprise system to supply its needs, except where it is in the national interest for the Government to provide directly the products and services it uses."[9] The message obtained from many sources is that government contracting is extensive, yet there is no handy information to show Congressman Kemp that contracting is, in fact, increasing.

Contracting and special authorities also have their critics. One specialist on authorities argues that they are innovative in raising money but conservative in spending it. Points of reference for authorities are more likely to be bankers than social groups.[10] In being autonomous, special authorities and contractors lack responsiveness to norms defined by the democratic process. Contractors and special authorities slight such values as affirmative action and a well-paid civil service. Contractors often pay less than the government for unskilled work, while they pay more than the government for professional and managerial tasks. The people who lose government jobs when an agency program goes to contractors are disproportionately the poor and members of minority groups. Sometimes contractors and special authorities are more expensive than government departments engaged in similar activities.

Government contracting with voluntary social service agencies raises its own variety of special problems. Some commentators worry about the domination of voluntary bodies by government, or the preemption by government of their activities. Government expenditures for a group of child-care-related programs grew by 650 percent from 1950 to 1970; comparable growth in the voluntary sector was only 200 percent.[11] Much of the increase in government spending funnels through voluntary agencies and makes them leading social service contractors in local communities. Some observers applaud the diversity in social service delivery achieved via contracting. Clients are freed from dependence on government agencies that monopolize service programs, and the clients may even benefit from competition between service providers.[12] Other observers focus on the dilemmas created by extensive contracting with voluntary agencies:[13]

Problems of coordination among separate agencies that deal in similar services in the same community

Challenges to the autonomy of voluntary agencies via mechanisms of governmental control

Lack of public control over the programs administered by voluntary agencies seeking to maximize their autonomy

Dilution of the benefits derived from voluntarism in social services, as agencies and their contributors come to rely on government contracts for the bulk of their funds

Problems of church-state separation, felt both by secular interests toward social service agencies having a religious sponsorship and by religious sponsors who feel the erosion of their traditional social service roles

Bodies on the margins have restive clients and encounter charges of discrimination, excessive charges, and improper treatment of clients. The managers of sheltered workshops that contract with government have been described in the *Wall Street Journal* as receiving high salaries and fringe benefits, while their handicapped personnel remain in low-paid menial jobs that do not offer meaningful instruction.[14] Officials in charge of a New York social service contractor were charged with the cruel and unusual punishment of children they placed in institutions.[15]

In speaking to a conference about the purchase of services in the health and welfare fields, George Wiley, executive director of the National Welfare Rights Organization, noted:

[There has been] relatively little insight as to exactly how the professional welfare worker fits into the ultimate scheme for the benefit of the poor people.... The things that are commonly defined as services by social workers, the things to which social workers devote so much attention and interest, are... apparently of little value to the people who are on welfare.[16]

The title and some chapter headings in a book published by the American Federation of State, County, and Municipal Employees signals that organization's feeling toward contracting. The book is called *Government for Sale: Contracting-Out the New Patronage*. Chapters include "Agnew: Symbol of the System"; "New York City: Contracting-Out Is Political Patronage"; "Getting Rich Off the Poor";

"Blue Collar Workers: The First to Go"; and "Managers Who Can't Manage."

In writing on contractors who consult about local planning, one critic notes, "Twenty years of Federal planning assistance programs have not built up the planning capacity of local governments or improved the quality of life. Indeed, the prime beneficiary of such aid seems to be neither local governments nor local residents, but local and national consultants."[17]

INCOHERENCE AS CAUSE AND EFFECT
ON THE MARGINS

The development of special authorities and government contracting has added to the incoherence of American government. Thanks to these two phenomena on the margins of the American state, more institutions and a greater variety of procedures now exist. However, both special authorities and contracting developed partly *because of* existing incoherence. Many special authorities facilitated state and local financing amid archaic constitutional provisions against borrowing. Others came on the scene because the proliferation of suburban governments made obstacle courses for local service delivery. With dozens of municipal governments dividing up the terrain of a metropolitan area, it is impossible to deliver services across a whole area without setting up special authorities. Water and sewage authorities, airport authorities, toll road authorities, and others provide services throughout the region, oblivious to central city and suburban boundaries.

One whole class of government contractors developed to help state and local authorities through the maze created by federal aid programs. For state and local governments on the receiving end of federal aid, the programs look as complex as the indecipherable bargain fares offered by the airlines. A long time ago, both airlines and passengers learned that they needed travel agents to help with the explanations and the paperwork. The same holds true in government. Donors and recipients employ firms of consultants to help them design and manage intergovernmental programs. Some of the contractors who work for recipients receive a percentage of the grant as their fee. On the Washington end, a number of firms that consult with federal agencies have located themselves in new office buildings on the circumferential highway. The trade calls them "Beltway Bandits" out of respect for their ability to help themselves while they help the government.

With many hundreds of separate federal-aid programs offering upward of $70 billion each year, the menu is too complex for state and local authorities to know their entitlements. Some consultants advise state or community officials as to the federal programs most suitable to their needs. Consultants also assemble materials for an application, and nurse the paperwork through the regional office and Washington headquarters of a federal department. Federal money is attractive but "soft." There is no guarantee that it will continue to flow beyond an initial term. For this reason, state and local officials are reluctant to add permanent staff for federally aided programs. It is safer to hire another contractor to provide the services paid for with the federal money. If the aid stops, the state or local agency can terminate its contract with the service provider without being responsible for its personnel. If the federally aided program calls for an evaluation, this also can be contracted. Firms experienced in this line of work claim to know what kind of evaluation is acceptable in Washington.

The programs of the U.S. Department of Health, Education, and Welfare typify the difficulties encountered with federal offerings. Many separate programs — 330 by one count — go from Washington headquarters to a variety of state or local agencies. HEW offers 12,000 pages of regulations and interpretive guidelines for its 330 programs. As viewed by recipients, all this detail forces recipients to concentrate on federal requirements at the expense of genuine innovation. At no point is there a mechanism to select from many particular program items those needed by individual clients. The agencies of state and local governments hire contractors to help them sort through HEW offerings. Individual clients of these programs, in contrast, may have no help. Yet the typical clients of a social service have neither the skill nor the temperament to negotiate a complex patchwork. One study finds that 86 percent of clients actually need more than one service. Three out of five persons who visit an office for a social service must go elsewhere because the agency they approach does not offer what they need.[18]

Requirements pertaining to contracting present their own maze, even though contracting promises to help officials cope with complexity. In 1976 the head of the Wisconsin Department of Administration asked the state's attorney general if the department was required by law to use the bidding process in purchasing the services of architectural and engineering consultants. The answer was a qualified yes, but it required a seven-page letter that cited twenty-eight sections or subsections of Wisconsin statutes plus four court decisions or opinions of the Legislative Reference Bureau.

Wisconsin's Division of Mental Health deals with sixty-two Community Service Boards throughout the state that arrange programs for mental illness, developmental disabilities, alcoholism, and drug abuse. Some 30 percent of their activities are contracted out, mostly to private agencies. In order to aid the boards in achieving uniform standards of services, costs, and recordkeeping, the Department of Health and Social Services produced an 81-page administrative order. Unfortunately, the technical language of the order was too complex for members of the Community Service Boards.[19]

In describing the margins of the American state,[20] two kinds of units attract our attention: special authorities and government contractors. One task of this chapter is to detail some of the differences between these bodies. At the same time, it is important to note their commonalities. Both special authorities and government contractors are independent of conventional governmental actors in the legislative and executive branches. Both special authorities and government contractors add to the system's complexity and weaken the capacity to shape public services via democratic politics. Yet both special authorities and contractors do a great deal of work that we think of as government work. Often they enjoy monopoly control over important services and rely, directly or indirectly, on the taxing powers of government.

THE AMERICAN SETTING

Institutions on the margins of the American state do not simply appear. They grow from national soil and reflect the political culture, economics, and government structure. In this general way they share the experiences of bodies marginal to Australia and Israel. The details differ according to the traits of each country.

Political Culture

The political culture of the United States has an antigovernmental strain that is largely absent from the cultures of either Australia or Israel. Proposition 13 — the California referendum that limits the taxation of real property by local governments — is the latest in a string of antitax, antigovernment expressions that dates back to the Boston Tea Party. The United States is suspicious of bureaucrats. At least since the time of Andrew Jackson, many Americans have felt that the work of government should be available to the common person, the individual without special skill or breeding. Much of Americans' fascination with creating governments expresses itself in devices to limit the power of government. Suburban municipalities sprang up to limit the spread of the central city, and to provide residents with independence. Many elections and referenda claim to keep the actions of government close to the people. Americans have resisted the European pattern of developing elite cadres of civil servants. The top jobs in national and state bureaucracies are open to outsiders. It is a virtue for business executives to come into government and keep the bureaucracy from becoming too inbred. Large numbers of people, often in positions of political influence, feel that private business is inherently more efficient than government. Circular A-76 of the U.S. Office of Management and Budget is an important indication of this. It directs federal departments to contract-out functions to the private sector whenever possible.

Along with this distrust of government, the American culture contains ingredients of individualism and entrepreneurialism. There are viable myths in the Yankee trader, Horatio Alger, and inventors like Edison and Bell who built giant industries. These traits liken American culture to the Israeli more than to the Australian. What distinguishes American culture from the Israeli is the American distrust of government. Israelis are individualistic and entrepreneurial, but they are also the first modern generation of Jews living under a Jewish government. In the eyes of many Israelis, their nation has a position close to veneration. In both the United States and Israel, there is ample room for an individual entrepreneur to develop a distinctive unit for the provision of a public service. In the Israeli context, the unit is likely to be a government company. In the United States, the unit is likely to be a private firm doing business with the state.

The Structure of Government

Influences on the margins of the American state also come from the structure of government. The United States is a federal system with distinct boundaries between the national government and the states. There is also a strong tradition of local autonomy, which creates power for municipalities and counties. All told, 21,500 general-purpose governments provide much opportunity for variation. The margins of the American state are wide, and they are home to many strange creatures. The peculiar histories of the national government and each state and municipality make themselves felt in the ways the margins have developed around each government. The heavy use of special authorities by state and local governments, for example, owes much to state experiences in the nineteenth century. Unwise and unethical state officers authorized huge borrowing for uneconomic public facilities; railroads and canals were built far beyond the capacity of state economies to generate sufficient traffic. Localities and state institutions spent a great deal of money on land and buildings, perhaps spending more on kickbacks to contractors and corrupt officials than on improving services. In response, reformers wrote strict prohibitions against borrowing into state constitutions. In the twentieth century, with growing populations and growing service demands, some way had to be found to get around those constitutional limitations. A popular invention was the special authority, enabled to borrow on its own name, outside the framework of state or local government.

Yet another incentive to the development of special authorities came from the proliferation of separate municipalities around the edges of great cities. Robert Wood's book about the New York metropolitan area, *1400 Governments*, conveyed an image of governmental surplus and complexity around most large American cities. Chicago boasts 1301 governments in its metropolitan area; St. Louis 483.

Beginning in the late 1940s, the problems of metropolitan areas became a favorite target of reformers. They cited a surplus of government as causing inefficiency and inequality in local services. Tax rates varied widely across the metropolis, as did opportunities for good schools, libraries, and effective police departments. Some people who paid the highest taxes suffered from the worst services. There were many efforts to merge cities and suburbs, but most failed. Suburbanites did not want to rejoin the city they had fled. Central-city political leaders did not want their constituencies diluted with the addition of suburbanites.[21] By the early 1970s, some intellectuals saw great merit in the variety of local government. They liked variation for the opportunities it provided residents and business firms to choose the kind of community they wanted, according to the package of taxes and services offered.[22] Special authorities offered pragmatic attractions for metropolitan areas. They permitted wide jurisdictions for individual services without upsetting city and suburban boundaries.

The separation of powers — the system of checks and balances — also affects the margins of the state. This distinctive American feature of government assures competition between executive and legislative branches. It creates many independent politicians who are not subject to discipline by party or governmental superiors. This means lots of politicians to be "paid off" by giving jobs to their supporters or putting a government project in their constituency. Patronage has long been a feature of American government, but now there is a new wrinkle. Contracting multiplies the goodies distributed. Members of Congress or the state legislature can be rewarded by throwing a government contract to their supporters. Rather than assign a new program to an existing agency, the program can be divided among lots of contracts. One contractor can design the program, several contractors can deliver services in different communities, and another contractor can monitor the program. What might have been assigned to one agency can be distributed to several firms or individuals, perhaps with the higher total cost justified by the alleged productivity of the private sector.

The Economy

The American economy also has some effect on the margins of the state. Not only do vast resources facilitate the multiplication of institutions but huge corporations stand ready to take advantage. Companies like Westinghouse, Lockheed, and I.T.T. produce hardware for the military, design social programs, deliver job training and counseling, clean government buildings, and serve food in government cafeterias. In the realm of special authorities, it is possible to find banks and insurance companies. They define obligations regarding the repayment of loans, and help to shape program details.

PLUSES AND MINUSES

One appeal of bodies on the margins in America is their diversity. This means flexibility. Policy makers can select precisely the kind of special authority or contract that seems suitable to their needs and fine-tune details of organizational structure, goals, and personnel. On the consumer's side, there can be multiple providers of a service within easy reach, especially in large cities. Even though the consumer does not have the wide selection policy makers encounter, some choice is better than none. To be sure, problems arise when there is great variety.

Policies are incoherent to all but the expert. The policy maker and the consumer need help to sort through the options. Diversity hinders program evaluation by common or clear standards. Yet, for all that, program diversity seems to complement all the other fascinating diversities that make up the American population.

Contracting

Flexibility is a general trait that contracting shares with other bodies on the margins of the state. Indeed, contracting may lend itself to more flexibility than any other mechanism considered in this book. A contract can be negotiated with great precision, in terms of a specific project or personnel, and for a limited period of time. Experimentation is one possibility, with the participants being careful to limit a contract's life to that period needed to design a program and gather information about its feasibility.

The University of Wisconsin's Institute for Research on Poverty, working with the U.S. Office of Economic Opportunity, administered an experimental program of guaranteed annual income and negative income tax for the marginal poor. The program ran for a limited time, and operated only in certain locales. Its primary purpose was not to aid clients but to examine their response to new techniques of income assistance. Would they become more dependent or less so? Would there be more incentive to work and become self-supporting, or less? Neither the national government nor the University of Wisconsin committed itself to continue this program beyond the contract term. No bureaucrats would be locked into a system with an incentive to keep it going forever. The research could lead to great changes in welfare administration, but changes would depend partly on the results of the experiment and partly on the interpretation of them by policy makers. In fact, the program led to no great changes in policy in the short run. Yet the findings have circulated widely among relevant groups of social scientists and welfare administrators and may affect policy changes in a more opportune climate.

The flexibility of contracting allows policy makers to offer services via small institutions, which are more likely to establish rapport with clients and deal responsively with their unique problems. The Wisconsin Division of Corrections contracts with several organizations that run halfway houses for from six to fourteen parolees. The Division of Vocational Rehabilitation contracts for counseling and job training.

Both divisions have programs to match individual clients with services available in the private sector, on a one-to-one basis. Contractors can be innovative in ways not likely to survive in a government office. One Wisconsin department contracted for services to high school dropouts prone to delinquency. The services included counseling, training in basic skills, and work discipline. Among the qualifications this contractor asked of potential counselors was the following: "in order to facilitate an effective working relationship with ex-offenders, the applicant should have some experience in confinement in a county jail or state correctional institution (although this is not required)."

Opponents cite the expense of these programs and instances of flagrant abuse. But this does not fault the principle of small group or individualized care. Accusations frequently deal with the careless use of techniques by case workers, or their lack of supervision by government agencies.

Any assessment of contracting must contrast the opportunities for doing good that result from its inherent flexibility with the opportunities for doing bad with the same flexibility. Many cases come close to the boundaries of good and bad. One state government engaged in a nationwide search for a new division chief, and in the early spring selected from another region a person with a national reputation. The job was to begin on July 1. The candidate wanted the job but found it awkward to wait several months to begin work and start receiving a salary. Also, there was the matter of moving expenses. A contract helped to solve these problems. The candidate accepted a consultant's contract until July 1, at a level of compensation sufficient to cover some costs of relocating. In this case, a contract allowed a state department to make its position more attractive to a person selected on the basis of stiff professional criteria. No personal favors were at stake, although there was a special deal outside the usual procedures and pay scale of the civil service.

Some contracts are arranged verbally; a memo in the files is the only record of the agreement. Wisconsin permits wide discretion to its administrative personnel for contracts under $3000; records of these agreements remain with the agency that initiates them. When executive or legislative attention turns to such contracts, it becomes difficult, if not impossible, to assemble the information for central review.

Procedures for arranging contracts permit great abuse. The General Accounting Office estimates that 85 percent of defense contracts and 71 percent of civilian contracts in sample years were not advertised and bid competitively.[23] Agency personnel identify a contractor they consider appropriate, and proceed to negotiate an agreement. The old saw that government equipment or services are chosen by price alone is often not true. There is opportunity for key administrators or elected office holders to steer contracts to friends, family members, party supporters, or firms allied with organized crime that threaten retribution if contracts do not come their way.

Critics charge that contracting does not offer all the flexibility claimed for it by its boosters. Start-up costs can be heavy. Capital-intensive contracts, ranging from those to produce armaments for the Defense Department to those to collect trash in a sizable city, require the purchase of equipment. A contract that deals in professional services, such as program evaluation, counseling, or medical care, may require an extensive staff. In order to justify start-up costs, potential contractors may demand a long-term arrangement. Once a deal is under way, it may not be possible to shift contractors even though a formal agreement is about to expire. New firms may not want to bid for a contract, fearing heavy start-up costs with only limited prospects for payoffs.

Contractors may use the old gimmick of the "introductory offer" or "loss leader" to win a contract. They then boost prices when a community has committed itself and closed the door to other options. Seattle residents found their charges for contracted trash collection increased by 93 percent between 1974 and 1976, from $2.70 to $5.35 per month.[24]

The quality and efficiency of contracting are not attributes that come automatically. Some claims of reduced costs are simply the product of reduced services. Trash pickup twice a week by a private contractor will be less expensive than three times a week by the city Department of Sanitation.

Both individuals and government agencies suffer from contractors who lessen the quality of their services below the levels specified in their contracts. Most vulnerable, perhaps, are people who are not sufficiently streetwise or aggressive to apply pressure successfully in the maze of contractors and government officials who respect contractors' autonomy. Even government agencies—presumably with the knowledge and resources to battle an irresponsible contractor—suffer from poor performance. A file of correspondence dealing with the contracted maintenance of a government building reveals lax control with respect to the cleaning of offices and public areas, as well as numerous incidents of petty vandalism and theft by employees of the contractor.

Officials seem to have accepted low-quality service rather than deal continually with the minimum-wage transients the contractor hired to do the work.

A memo from the nursing director of a state institution for the retarded complained about a contractor's laundry service in the most homely of terms:

> *Their work on the whole is almost totally unacceptable. I'm sure most of us as private citizens wouldn't tolerate for one minute sending our laundry out and getting it back like this without complaining and demanding immediate remedial action....*
>
> *Many of the items sent to the laundry are never returned.... Laundry received on the cottage is often not for that cottage and must be resorted. It isn't at all unusual to find laundry from such places as Lake Geneva Bunny Club, Marriott Inn, Holiday Inn, etc. Laundry comes back wet and mildewy — smelly.*

Even people who generally support contracting worry about the role of private interests in tasks of policy making that rightfully belong to elected officials. Circular A-76 of the U.S. Office of Management and Budget directs government agencies to rely "on the private enterprise system to supply its needs." Yet the circular exempts "these basic functions of management which [executive agencies] must perform in order to retain essential control over the conduct of their programs."[25] The problem arises near the thin line that separates policy advice from enactment. It is legitimate for government agencies to buy advice from outside contractors. According to Representative Patricia Schroeder (D-Colo.), however, "so often what happens is that by the time the study has been contracted out, it's very hard to overcome that expert label, and very often there have been indications that there have been potential conflicts of interest."[26]

Conflict of interest is a frequent companion of contracting. At times the conflict is blatant and criminal. Former Vice President Spiro Agnew is only the most prominent of many officials who have lost their positions, paid fines, or served time in jail for receiving bribes, kickbacks, or other improper favors from contractors. An assistant U.S. attorney general estimates that one thousand federal, state, and local officials were convicted of felonies from 1970 to 1976. A high incidence of these convictions touched on government contracts with private firms.[27]

More recently, American news media have explored dealings between employees of the U.S. General Services Administration and contractors. Certain employees have used government purchase orders either to buy things for their personal use or for illegal resale. Others have accepted grossly inflated contractors' claims to have delivered goods or services. One stairwell in a government office building appeared on the network news several nights running. According to invoices, it had been painted many times over a short period. Yet visual inspection showed nothing like the good treatment the government had paid for.

Some contracting that is not outright crooked is made suspect by cozy dealing. Contractors work both for a government agency and for business firms subsidized or regulated by the agency. Peat, Marwick, Mitchell, a large accounting and management consulting firm, was simultaneously a contractor for the U.S. Department of Transportation and Penn Central. The contractor was asked by DOT to help determine how to account for Metroliner costs when the government subsidized Penn Central's operation of the train. Later, Penn Central's bankruptcy was the subject of investigations by the Securities and Exchange Commission and Congress. Part of the inquiries focused on misleading reports about Penn Central's financial condition. According to Wright Patman, chairman of the House Banking and Currency Committee, "Information in the Committee's possession shows that this policy of 'doctoring' the financial statements was done at the direction of top Penn Central officials. These documents further indicate that Peat, Marwick, Mitchell and Co. played a substantial role in these successful attempts to misinform the investing public."[28]

At times, one arm of government rips off another via contracting. State governments have learned to write contracts from one state agency to another in order to make it look like one of them is spending money for services. This is reported to Washington as the state's contribution to a federal-state program, and draws federal aid on a matching basis. With this gimmick, Illinois boosted its receipts of social service grants by almost twice the national average over the 1971-73 period, and caused a bureaucratic furor that reached the President's desk. Illinois also taught New York State how to do it, and New York increased its federal receipts even more than Illinois.[29]

New York City also used contracting to evade conditions imposed by federal and state government when they helped the city out of its scrape with bankruptcy in 1975-76. The city met the conditions by laying off workers on the one hand while contracting out services on the other hand.[30]

Special Authorities

Special authorities offer their own flexibility, and their own problems of assessment. For many years, New Jersey had no adequate revenue source. There was no retail sales tax or individual income tax, the two sources most state governments use to collect the bulk of their revenue. New Jersey's largest source of state revenue was the gasoline tax. A state with a population as large, sophisticated, and demanding as New Jersey's needed a great deal more money. Like many universities, Rutgers — The State University used the mechanism of special authorities to borrow for dormitories and cafeterias, with the proceeds from those services being used to pay off the bonds. In this way the state could build without spending its own money. Where Rutgers went beyond the general pattern was to put classrooms on the ground floors of dormitories. Dormitory residents thus paid for classrooms along with their room rent.

Many of the facilities New Yorkers use for transportation and recreation came from the creativity, the arrogance, and the independence Robert Moses demonstrated as chairman of several state and city authorities. Jones Beach and the parkways New Yorkers drive along to get to the outer reaches of Long Island are the creations of Moses, as are the Triborough, the Verrazano-Narrows, and the Bronx Whitestone bridges, the West Side Highway, the Hutchinson River Parkway, vast improvements in Central Park, and the creation of a thousand other parks. These would not, in all probability, have been constructed in anything like their present form by conventional departments of government. Moses benefited from his independence of the legislature, the city council, the governor, and the mayor. He could use the weight of bond dealings and construction, architectural, and consulting contracts as patronage to smooth his projects, without becoming the tool of some politician's patronage needs. He produced results, quickly, and often at a quality beyond that of the customary products of government. Politicians came to accept his arrogance because he had the public and the press on his side. He was building what people wanted, and he was a political force in his own right. The end came for Moses only with advancing age, and to some extent with a change in the public's support for massive public works. Before that time came, however, Moses had used several authorities over a forty-year span to remake the physical reality of a great city.[31]

Special authorities can operate more efficiently than government agencies. Authority managers are more free than their counterparts in the agencies to hire, promote, or fire staff with an eye to productivity.

Salaries in authorities may be higher than those in government, and they thus facilitate the selection of good employees. Authority tasks may be simpler than those of government, and may contribute to "businesslike" management. Progress toward the construction of roads, bridges, or dormitories can be charted more clearly and good work rewarded more directly than for the programs of a social agency.[32] All of which is to find some merit in the stereotypes boasted by authority supporters, but to place them in the context of the kinds of activities authorities perform.

One of the keys to Robert Moses's career as head of the Triborough Bridge and Tunnel Authority was his reliance on contracting. Unlike many units of government, the authority faced no requirements for competitive bidding. Because of Moses's monopoly on lucrative segments of the transportation market, he could be less concerned about costs than could many private businessmen. His select and loyal group of contractors worked at great speed, and kept Moses in the headlines as a spectacular producer of public works.

The work of authorities, like that of contractors, may evoke applause or criticism. To some extent, it depends on who is being served. A subsidiary of the Port Authority of New York and New Jersey created the World Trade Center. This did more for lower Manhattan than it did for mass transit, which is where the authority's critics thought the transport-oriented authority should have put the money. Across the Hudson River, the New Jersey Highway Authority built the Garden State Arts Center, which also seemed a bit removed from that authority's principal mission of transportation.[33]

CONTROLLING THE MARGINS

The diversity of special authorities and government contractors in the United States makes them hard to control. Australians and Israelis have an easier time with the margins of their countries. Even though Australian statutory authorities and Israeli government companies differ in details from one to another, in each country one legal format rules for most bodies on the margins of those states. There is a wider variety of special authorities in the United States, and a virtually infinite variety of government contractors. Moreover, the competition built into policy making in the United States—between members and agents of separate executive and legislative branches—further complicates control over the margins.

Contractors

The procedures for arranging contracts are a government's first line of defense in the process of control. Although the procedural details of contracting vary greatly from one jurisdiction to another, they tend to share the following traits:

1. General guidelines, proclaimed by the chief executive. These may specify a general policy toward contracting-out or in-house activities, specify a central unit (perhaps a unit of the budget bureau or a separate procurement agency) that has general charge of contracting, indicate the steps to be followed in clearing a contract with this central agency, and specify a monetary value of small contracts that agencies may arrange on their own without central clearance.

2. Standard formats promulgated by the central unit given general responsibility for contract supervision. These may include a questionnaire that asks an operating agency to justify contracting, perhaps in terms of elaborate costing calculations, and specify procedures for selecting a specific contractor. These procedures may begin with public advertisements and formal bidding by prospective contractors, but are likely to allow negotiated contracts (i.e., agreements made between government agencies and firms chosen on some other basis than formal bids). For such negotiations to proceed, the government agency may require written approval from a key official, perhaps the chief executive. In like manner, the standard formats may require a contractor's acceptance of the government's policies toward affirmative action hiring of minorities, women, and the handicapped; may specify that potential contractors located in the government's jurisdiction will be given preference over outsiders; and may outline procedures for auditing the performance of contractors. With each requirement, however, there may be procedures for excusing a particular contract on the written approval of some key official of government.

In judging the procedures for controlling contractors, it is essential to distinguish actual practice from formal rules. Exceptions seem to be freely allowed, especially for negotiating contracts outside the advertising-bidding procedure. There may be only loose steps for screening these exceptions, with central government officers routinely signing requests without inquiring into their justification. Moreover, the categories of small contracts — a dollar figure below which there is little or no central clearance — are widely used. If the limit is $3000 (as it is in Wisconsin), many contracts come in between $2900 and $3000. At times, projects are divided into several components with each component fitting under the limit that allows an agency to make arrangements on its own.

The vast numbers of separate contracts have something to do with the problems of control. Wisconsin has shown modest enthusiasm for contracting. A spurt of public interest in the spring of 1978 came with the news that some $62.4 million (less than 5 percent of the amount for state government operations) was spent on contractual services during the preceding fiscal year. Interest heated up, and a Committee of the Legislature sought information on contracting. It was told that "it would take 3 to 5 months of searching to obtain the data . . . just for the Departments of Natural Resources and Health and Social Services and the University of Wisconsin. . . . It would involve searching through 1.5 million documents, and . . . the documents we sought were not available by category . . . the data obtained would probably be incomplete, if it could be found at all."[34]

In response to the legislature's request, administrative departments made some effort to cull information on contracting from 1973 to 1978. The deputy secretary of the Department of Health and Social Services sent out a memo to his division administrators that reflected something other than a burning desire to cooperate:

> The Legislative Joint Committee on Review of Administrative Rules has requested the Department to provide them with the information listed on the attached. After reviewing this, you will realize, I am certain, that this is an almost impossible task.
>
> In an attempt to reduce this task to more manageable proportions, we are going to provide the Committee with a list of the types of contracts we have in the Department, and hopefully convince them that representative samples of the different types would be sufficient. . . .[35]

A mixed bag of information came to the department in response to this memo. Two divisions sent in handwritten lists of contracts. One listed a random sample of voucher payments including only the voucher number and the amount of payment, with no reference to the service being purchased or the name of the contractor. Another sent a ten-page list of contractors' names with no identification of the nature of services being purchased.

Federal controls over contractors are also thin. While there is an abundance of control agencies and regulations, weaknesses appear at the working level. Each of several controllers takes a narrow view of its responsibilities and seems willing to overlook obvious problems that it can define as outside its province. The Merit System Protection Board — a spinoff from the former Civil Service Commission — has a role in certain matters dealing with government employees affected by contracting, but it does not concern itself with defining costs or savings accruing from a reduction of the government work force because of contracting. Moreover, the board does no systematic checking on contracting by agencies. It waits on agency requests or until a complaint is filed by an employee who alleges improper treatment.[36]

The Office of Management and Budget has one unit within it — the Office of Federal Procurement Policy — that handles a range of issues involved in contracting. A report it issued in 1976 dealt with numerous activities. Some appeared simple, such as the purchase by the Department of Agriculture of twine (i.e., string) from non-U.S. suppliers in violation of "Buy American" requirements. Other activities seemed weightier, such as improving procedures for acquiring new systems, based on a more explicit simplification of mission needs (i.e., end results to be accomplished) than had been the case previously.

The Office of Management and Budget also has the responsibility for checking comparative cost figures on contracting-out versus doing a service in-house. But this extends only to new activities. Asked at a congressional hearing about a general program to analyze costs for established programs that are contracted-out, an OMB executive said, "There is no requirement and no desire that any of these actions be reviewed by the Office of Management and Budget."[37]

The General Accounting Office, an audit body accountable to Congress, has a general mandate to review contracting but has no power to halt actions that go contrary to its preferences. GAO can halt spending only for those activities that run counter to *explicit legislation.* Furthermore, the GAO has shown little interest in contracting as a general problem. Its typical treatment deals with contracting along with other issues in the administration of particular programs.

Late in 1978 the GAO released a study on the administration of contracts and grants. The grants involved dealings between federal agencies and state and local governments. The GAO found grant and contract administration to be lax on several grounds. Unfortunately, the mixture of grants and contracting in the same study blurred any possibility of learning about the distinctive problems of each. At the time of the study, some $4.3 billion in outstanding cases were being contested, with about 80 percent of that figure potentially recoverable by the U.S. Treasury. Some cases had been dragging on for ten years. As an indication of its lack of enforcement power, the GAO noted that agency administrators have the final word on issues of questionable expenditures. Yet administrators consider the resolution of these issues to be onerous, and therefore give them low priority.

The number of control units with a role in contract supervision is one reason why contractors have autonomy. The federal government assigns the major role in contract matters to the operating agency. There has also been an Office of Contract Compliance that checks contractors with respect to general policies like affirmative action, as well as the Merit System Protection Board, the Office of Management and Budget, and the General Accounting Office. State governments have parallel bodies. Chief executives and legislative committees have general responsibilities to deal with issues of contracting. With different actors in the play, each has some concern to avoid offending the others. This is particularly true when issues of federal-state relations combine with issues of contracting. State officials give low priority to the review of contracts that state agencies purchase with federal money. Federal control units would rather not look too closely at activities implemented by state or local agencies. It is similar to the rules found in Australia with respect to federal-state programs or in Israel regarding the joint ventures of a government company: if a control unit can find a reason *not* to look at a project involving more than one government entity, it will take advantage of that reason. To do otherwise would be to risk a jurisdictional battle with a jealous neighbor on the governmental terrain, and would fritter away time and energy that are already in too short supply to deal thoroughly with problems that are clearly one's own responsibility.

The most important actors in the contracting game are the contractors and the personnel of government agencies who arrange contracts. In a setting where the bulk of contracts are negotiated, rather than bid secretly and competitively, a key item is the knowledge contractors and agencies have of one another. It is important for the contractor to know the techniques, concepts, and "buzzwords" (faddish shorthand for problems or services) that are currently in favor. Potential contractors cultivate contacts with agency personnel to gain information about what an agency wants, and how much it can spend. Often a contractor helps shape the agency's definition of what it wants — and not surprisingly the shape is in the direction of what that contractor can provide. At times the contractor is also the agency person. Governments permit contracts to their own employees, with more or less stringent protections to assure that the work is done after hours and is outside the boundaries of the employee's full-time job with the government. Contracts also come from the ranks of agency alumni. Employees learn they can do better on the outside peddling their talent to former colleagues who remain on the inside.

Contractors take steps to enhance their access to government. The crudest of their techniques can result in disgrace and incarceration for government officials on the take. Also of interest are subtle payoffs, where the beneficiaries seem to be receiving nothing more than an honor. Some of the more prominent nonprofit bodies, such as United Fund and church or ethnic welfare agencies, recruit members of their boards of directors from government units that make decisions about contracts. This can be looked on as nothing more than an honorary appointment, innocent at least at first glance. Such directors may actually participate in policy making for the nonprofit organization, or may simply lend their name and prestige in exchange for the prestige of being a director of the charity. Yet charities and other prestigious public bodies have become important figures in contracting. Contracts of the Wisconsin Department of Health and Social Services include the YMCA, an affiliate of the NAACP, Lutheran Social Services, Jewish Vocational Services, Great Lakes Inter-Tribal Council, Inc., Goodwill Industries, the Urban League, and the St. Vincent De Paul Society. To the extent that government officials with a role in contracting also have a role in the direction of contractors there is a conflict of interest under Wisconsin law.[38]

In 1978 the Wisconsin Department of Health and Social Services appointed a citizens' committee to oversee a survey of its contracting. Either through innocence or guile, the foxes were set to count the chickens. Most original members of the citizens' committee were officials of nonprofit organizations that serve as contractors.

At times there is conflict between government agents and contractors. As noted earlier, the Wisconsin Division of Corrections contracts extensively for halfway houses, counseling, training, and health services for parolees and probationers. In all these services problems arise between contractors and parole agents on the division's staff.

Contractors discourage involvement in their activities by parole agents. Agents work with higher case loads as a result of purchasing services from contractors, and find some problem in defining their roles between supervising or assisting parolees. Parole agents outside Milwaukee note that the metropolitan region has only 38 percent of the state's cases but gets 73 percent of the contracts for services.[39]

Unions of government employees are prominent critics of contracting. Their activity is vocal and occasionally productive. The Wisconsin State Employees Union claims to have altered a decision by the state's Department of Administration to contract-out maintenance services for several state office buildings. It did this by convincing the legislature's Joint Finance Committee that the Department of Administration's cost analysis was faulty. The government's argument rested on contractors that paid lower wages than the state. The government's argument did not take sufficient account of the costs in unemployment compensation or social services to be received by government employees laid off as a result of contracting.[40]

Recent commentators emphasize the growth in contracting. Many attribute this to the spurt in social programs begun during the Johnson administration's war on poverty. A great deal of contracting is prompted by federal programs. States and localities are loath to expand their permanent staffs for a federally funded program. In fact, federal aids have climbed sharply since 1965; they grew by 356 percent between 1965 and 1975, 130 percent faster than government revenues.

Claims about the newness of contracting must be viewed with caution. Back in 1961, the Government Employees Council of the AFL-CIO noted that it was "gravely concerned over the growing practice in the Federal service, to contract to private interests, certain governmental services and functions that have historically been performed by civil service employees."[41] At about the same time, an interagency committee of the U.S. government raised some basic issues about the control of contractors. In a report to the President, the committee expressed concern about the capacity of government officials to oversee contractors adequately and maintain control over basic policies. In response to this report, a spokesman for the contractors raised the issue of excessive control by government agencies over contractors.[42] Thus, the central issues about contractor control versus autonomy were clearly defined years ago. If there has been a subsequent spurt in contracting, its precise magnitude is not known. It is also not clear that such a spurt has altered the character of relations between the core units of government and the margins of the state.

Politicking about Contracting

Government contracting is a live issue in the United States. Key officials have been moved to examine and clarify their policies. Their tasks are not made easier by the lack of systematic information about contracting available to key officials of both federal and state governments. Examinations begin from the perspectives of different policies toward contracting. The national government has favored contracting whenever feasible; Wisconsin's present policy tilts against contracting.

Circular A-76 of the Office of Management and Budget has defined the pro-contracting policy of the national government since 1967. The circular was modified in the years from 1976 to 1978, but not in a manner to alter policy in a substantial way. It will "continue to support the policy that the Government should rely on the private sector for goods and services...."[43] Yet the procedures for costing the advantages of contracting-out versus in-house activities are to be made more precise, and greater concern is to be shown for government employees who may be affected by the contracting.

In the details of the 1976-78 review of contracting procedures, it is possible to see one small point in policy that has crucial impact. The issue is the cost of government retirement programs to be used in assessing in-house versus contracting-out. The true cost of government retirement plans is elusive; it depends on unknown future events, such as inflation and the generosity of Congress to pensioners. Because both inflation and congressional generosity have been considerable in recent years, the cost of government pensions — and thereby the long-run cost of retaining government employees — can escalate *after* a decision is made to perform a service in-house. *The higher the cost figure assigned to government retirement costs, the more likely that a comparison will favor contracting-out a service.*

Between August 1976 and April 1978 the figure to be used for government retirement costs moved back and forth with all the marks of a pressure contest between contractors on one side and government employees' unions on the other. In August 1976 President Ford's Office of Management and Budget announced that "new guidance... for calculating overhead costs of commercial and industrial activities of the federal government could result in substantially greater use of the private sector, and lower costs."[44] What followed was an increase from 7 to 24.7 percent in the overhead factor for retirement benefits. This would put an additional 17.7 cents on each federal payroll dollar when comparing prices with private contractors.

The language and calculations of the Office of Management and Budget shifted with the advent of the Carter administration. OMB's language showed more awareness of government employees' interests by June of 1977, and its calculations dropped from 24.7 to 14.1 percent of payroll for retirement costs. In November 1977 OMB's figure moved upward to 20.4 percent of payroll for retirement costs. While the result bears all the signs of a compromise, OMB tried to legitimize it with the names of brother agencies: "This factor was produced by the Civil Service Commission's actuarial model, as modified and validated by the General Accounting Office, using current economic assumptions supplied by the Council of Economic Advisers."[45]

Wisconsin's policy tilts away from contracting. A modest storm brewed about the state capital in the spring and summer of 1978 over some $62.4 million in contractual services, which was less than 5 percent of state spending on its own activities. Strictly comparable figures are not available from Washington. Nevertheless, it is said that contracting by the national government amounts to one third the value of work done in-house. Within agencies like HEW, contracting is substantially greater than the work done in-house.

The details of administration are more discouraging to contracting in Wisconsin than in the national government. Wisconsin government agencies have substantial discretion only for contracts under $3000. Above that figure it is necessary to enter more elaborate controls involving the Department of Administration and even the governor. In the national government, however, agency personnel have substantial discretion for contracts up to $50,000.

The Wisconsin executive reacted to the contract tempest of 1978 by deciding to review all agency service contracts. According to a directive issued by Martin Schreiber, acting governor in 1978, administrative personnel were to determine if the capability to perform the contract service existed in the state government, and they were to tighten procedures for monitoring contractors' performance. Within the directive is language suggesting a continuing bias in favor of in-house service provision. Whether this continues will depend partly on the policy of the new governor, Lee Dreyfus, and partly on incentives to contract-out that will come along with federal aid.

Special Authorities

Information about government control of special authorities suggests that the authorities are at least as independent as contractors – and perhaps more so, insofar as the authorities have continuing rights to borrow money or allocate the revenues from their facilities. As long as authorities can support themselves financially, they are pretty much on their own.

Several forms of government control over special authorities exist on paper, but they seem to be loosely employed in practice. Boards of directors, who may be appointed by the governor or some other elected officeholder, seem to exercise no more substantial control over the management of special authorities than do corporation boards of directors over their managers. Government auditors provide another opportunity for supervision. Their scrutiny can range from the financial records of authorities to the effectiveness of program design and implementation. At the national level, the General Accounting Office does examine authorities outside government departments and agencies. In the states, however, where special authorities have developed most extensively, auditing has not followed the GAO model. There may be requirements for authorities to submit annual reports, but most states do not specify the format of these reports or assign audit personnel to review them.[46]

State legislatures have formal responsibility over special authorities. The legislatures are the source of acts that create authorities, and they can always take the initiative of reviewing authorities with an eye to changing the statutes. The general pattern, however, is for a legislature to tolerate the independence of an authority after the initial statute has been passed. Most legislatures allow local governments to establish authorities on their own; they do not have to apply to the legislature in each case.

State courts have the responsibility for keeping special authorities within the confines of the law. A challenge to a special authority may come to the courts from an aggrieved employee, a client, or a competitor. Authority executives generate their own cases before the courts in order to clarify the limits of their powers. For the most part, the courts have been permissive in their interpretation of the statutes. Courts have held that general statutes dealing with administrative control *do not* apply to the authorities. Authorities are held *not to be governmental subdivisions*, and they have been excluded from one-man, one-vote standards that apply to governments. Elections dealing with authority matters can be conducted on the basis of a property franchise, with individuals and corporations casting votes in proportion to their holdings. In the eyes of the courts, special authorities really are on the margins — or beyond the margins — of the American state.

The limited research done on special authorities suggests that they are dominated by their chief executives. Yet these executives vary greatly in style. Just within New York City, contrasts between the styles of Robert Moses and Austin J. Tobin fit the models of the *politico* and the *technocrat* introduced in the chapter on Australia. Moses was a wheeler-dealer who cultivated his image in the media as The Man Who Got Things Done. He used his public standing to bully elected officials of local, state, and sometimes national governments. At the height of his powers, his demonstrations of temper and threats to resign could wring concessions when rational argument failed.

Austin J. Tobin, by contrast, was a technocrat. He spent his entire career of forty-four years with the Port Authority of New York and New Jersey. Like Moses, he wanted complete control over this organization, which he headed for thirty years. Yet he sought to keep authority personnel free from external influences, and abjured Moses's style of using patronage to create support among builders, architects, and engineers. Tobin cultivated a reputation for firing personnel engaged in corrupt practices or supporting political candidates. He discouraged the efforts of outsiders to have certain persons hired. Threats of resignation were not his stock in trade. Tobin did resign in 1972, however, when he felt board members involved themselves too much in the management of the Port Authority.

If Robert Moses is a striking example of the politician-entrepreneur as a leader of special authorities, the career of Nelson Rockefeller shows how another variety of politician-entrepreneur might control authorities from the center of government. Rockefeller was ambitious for himself and for his state. He had the good fortune of becoming governor in a state — New York — that provides its chief executive with greater formal powers than those enjoyed by most other governors. Rockefeller combined these formal powers with a feeling for leadership that allowed him to maximize the potential of his office. He also exploited his extraordinary personal advantages. His contacts — and those of his family — over a long life in public affairs and business provided extensive leads for policy advice and recruits for top jobs. Rockefeller dipped into his impressive private funds to attract the persons he wanted to oversee important authorities, and to give his team some independence from salary scales and procedures defined in state law or regulations.

Much of what Rockefeller did as governor occurred via state authorities or corporations he established and sought to control. For the people to lead or control these authorities, he sought out other entrepreneurial personalities, who could be counted on for their personal loyalty. William J. Ronan, for one, served Rockefeller as head of the governor's program office and as a major figure in the Metropolitan Transit Authority, the New York Port Authority, and the Power Authority of New York State. Ronan has been described as "bright, blunt, totally unbeholden to anyone but the Governor . . . ruthless and impatient with the normal procedures of democracy." By one estimate, Rockefeller's private gifts to Ronan amounted to $650,000.[47]

A SUMMARY WORD ABOUT
MANAGEMENT AND ACCOUNTABILITY

Of the three countries considered in this book, the United States seems to have the most complex government and the greatest variety of organizations on the margins of the state. Basic features of federalism plus executive-legislative competition set the context for proliferating organizations; the great wealth of the United States provides the wherewithal. Negative feelings toward government in general and the civil service in particular assure that social welfare in the United States will come partly from organs dressed up to look like private enterprise even though they operate on the basis of government authority and resources. The uncounted special authorities and government contractors that produce so much of American-style socialism are on the margins of the state. To a great extent they run themselves, independent of serious control by elected officials or core agencies of government. There are hardly more than rough estimates about the extent of contracting or special authorities. When an occasional spurt of attention forces a review of government policy, changes in activity appear more cosmetic than real.

Political accountability must go begging in the United States. *Accountability to whom?* is a question that defies a simple answer. Independent executives and legislatures compete with one another over control of policy. Contrary directives allow managers of special authorities or contractors to cite confusion among controllers as an excuse for complying with nothing but their own desires. Even when members of the same political party control both houses of a legislature and the chief executive, the lack of party discipline means that factions or independent members in each branch can balk at any control over an errant contractor or special authority. The boundaries dividing federal, state, and local governments from one another and their respective authorities and contractors raise additional questions about accountability. The money to pay for most public services comes from different levels of government. In the United States, as in Australia and Israel, joint ventures encourage buck-passing among potential controllers and leave program managers on the margins of governmental attention.

Political scientists in the United States have gone no further in studying organizations on the margins of the state than have their colleagues in Australia or Israel. In all three societies, enormous resources and profound decisions take shape on the margins. This book can just begin the task of charting what happens there. That we do not know more is truly an intellectual crisis.

5

LESSONS
FROM
THE
MARGINS
OF
THE
STATE

The chapters about Australia, Israel, and the United States dealt with features that seldom occupy the attention of political scientists. Yet the margins are becoming larger than the state. In Victoria, Australia, statutory authorities on the margins are demonstrably larger than conventional departments of the state government. In Israel and the United States there are no adequate records by which to assess the full magnitude of government corporations, special authorities, or government contractors. Nevertheless, we know that such bodies are large and important. Here and there it seems that they are larger than conventional departments of the government. Yet, for observers and policy makers, the marginal character of these bodies helps to obscure them.

The proliferation of administrative entities seems to be a universal feature of welfare states, even as a welfare state seems to be a universal feature of well-to-do countries. With many organizations designing and providing public services, there is a general problem of incoherence. Neither policy makers nor clients know for sure who is entitled to receive what from which entity of the state. Much proliferation of administrative bodies has occurred on the margins of the state. Conventional policy makers concede that they cannot deal with all that the state is expected to do. Putting things on the margins saves time and trouble for conventional policy makers. At the same time, units placed on the margins of the state only worsen the problems of incoherence.

In order to make the point that incoherence has national varieties as well as a universal appearance, chapters 2-4 looked closely at the margins of three countries: Australia, Israel, and the United States. The evidence is illustrative more than exhaustive, but it shows linkages between the activities that occur on the margins of a state and the underlying traits of national culture, economics, and structure of government.

A SYNOPSIS OF NATIONAL TRAITS

There are lessons both for the policy maker and the political scientist on the margins of the state. Both groups need to understand what has become an important aspect of policy design and delivery. The policy maker has the additional obligation to move from an understanding to an improvement of resource utilization and program management. Table 2 summarizes much of what has been presented in chapters 2-4 about the cultures, economies, and government structures of three states, and how the organizations on their margins reflect these national traits.

Australia has a law-abiding and nonentrepreneurial culture that supports a compliant, passive attitude among its public servants. It is common for individuals to spend an entire career within a single organization. Australian executives fit well within the framework of statutory authorities, where the statute is the principal mechanism of government control. An affluent economy supports high levels of service quality and provides amenities for employees. The federal structure of government produces statutory authorities in state governments as well as on the Commonwealth level.

A major attraction on the margins of the Australian state is the public nature of controls. Statutes enacted by state or Commonwealth Parliaments permit public scrutiny and comment. On the negative side, the unique and detailed nature of the statutes (there are over eighty in Victoria alone) provides effective autonomy to the executives of each authority. The harsh realities compromise the political accountability that seems at first sight to be part of the statutory linkages between the core and margins of the state.

Israeli culture is aggressive and entrepreneurial, and supports a wider role for the state than appears in Australia. Moreover, the Israeli culture is more heterogeneous than the Australian. Even though

TABLE 2: Summary of National Traits and the Margins of Three States

	Australia	Israel	United States
Culture	law-abiding, careerist, homogeneous; intermediate state role	aggressive, entrepreneurial, heterogeneous; large state role	aggressive, entrepreneurial, heterogeneous; free enterprise
Economy	wealthy	strained	wealthy
Government structure	federal without local autonomy; parliamentary	unitary; parliamentary with parallel structures of Labor Federation, Jewish Agency	federal with local autonomy; separation of powers; many centers of power
Prevailing mode of units on the margin	statutory authority	government and/or Labor Federation and/or Jewish Agency participation in limited liability companies	special authorities and government contractors
Principal means of control	statutory language	appointees to boards of directors, activist ministries and State Comptroller, aggressive press	variety of executive and legislative bodies, legislative committee hearings, aggressive media
Attractive features	public nature of policy and control instrument; high level of compliance and service quality	entrepreneurial managers allow stretching of strained resources; entrepreneurial control agents counter entrepreneurial managers	flexibility of administrative forms and services; accommodations with lack of governmental integration in metropolitan areas and with archaic limitations against government borrowing
Unattractive features	specificity of statutes limits inputs from core government and compromises political accountability gained by having statutes public	mixed quality of services, lack of manageability; extensive subsidiaries and joint ventures compromise political accountability by being (in practice) outside network of control	lack of effective accountability due to number and diversity of organs on the margin, lack of discipline among controllers of executive and legislative branches, and extensive federal-state-local joint ventures; incidence of patronage; wasteful, low quality or ineffective services

both are immigrant societies, Israel's population has more diverse origins, and no single national group has been critical in creating the society. A combination of more aggressive managers and a more diverse culture makes the Israeli scene less coherent than the Australian. Moreover, the structure of government in Israel adds to the diversity and complexity. Although the formal government structure is unitary — and thereby simpler than Australia's federalism — the reality of Israeli government is an amalgam of three public sectors. There is much overlapping of personnel and many joint ventures between the government, the Labor Federation, and the Jewish Agency.

The prevailing organization on the margins of the Israeli state is suited to mixed ownership. The government, the Labor Federation, and the Jewish Agency each use the format of the limited-liability company for their ventures. They appoint company directors to the extent of their shareholdings in company stock. General company law leaves the directors and managers free to create subsidiaries and joint ventures. The capital for these ventures may come from any of the parent bodies (government, Labor Federation, or Jewish Agency) or may be raised from other investors in Israel or abroad. The government relies heavily on its appointees to company boards of directors in order to control these firms plus the personnel of government control units such as the Finance Ministry and the State Comptroller. Control officers of the government are encouraged to be as entrepreneurial in controlling public corporations as corporate managers are likely to be entrepreneurial in expanding their organizations. An important supplement to the government's control efforts is an aggressive press, which is unhindered in its exposés by anything as strict as Australia's libel law.

Entrepreneurialism is the principal attraction on the margins of the Israeli state. Ambitious managers help a small country stretch its strained economy to cover a full range of domestic services, as well as massive defense obligations. Entrepreneurial control agents maintain some order in public corporations. They have learned all the tricks of spinning off subsidiaries and joint ventures. Personnel of the Israeli Finance Ministry and State Comptroller express aesthetic pleasure in the discovery of new schemes, even while they seek to plumb their depths in order to learn what is happening with public resources. Just as entrepreneurial company managers hope to advance their careers by doing something spectacular, so entrepreneurial control agents in the government hope to advance their careers by spotting an ingenious but irresponsible use of public resources.

The margins of the Israeli state also expose a negative side. Service quality is uneven. Segments of the public sector—organized as joint ventures or municipal corporations—are virtually autonomous from central supervision. Uneven service quality is partly a product of organizational confusion. The integrity of ministerial control over government companies, or a company's own control over its subsidiaries, suffers amid the scrambling of entrepreneurial managers to advance their careers. The economy also has something to do with the uneven service quality. Israel is significantly less wealthy than either Australia or the United States. External problems of defense and internal ambitions for a full-service social state stretch limited resources so that gaps must show.

The culture of the United States resembles that of Israel more than that of Australia. There is a strong component of individualism and Yankee entrepreneurship in American folklore and reality. Unlike Israel, this feature of American culture combines with an antigovernment strain. In spite of the creation of an extensive and generous welfare state, the United States exhibits some throwbacks to an earlier age. For example, Proposition 13 reflects an antigovernmental trend begun with the Boston Tea Party, continued in the Whiskey Rebellion, and kept alive in periodic defeats of school bond issues. Antigovernment rhetoric figures prominently in justifying units on the margins of the American state.

Heterogeneity is also a trait of the American culture. Regional differences have been prominent from the nation's beginning. This heterogeneity joins the federal nature of government and the honored place given local autonomy in supporting much governmental diversity. Wealth also has something to do with this; the United States has never been so hard pressed financially as to check its propensity toward making more governments. There are some 21,500 general-purpose governments: national, state, counties, and municipalities. Each government has spawned its own units on the margins. There are uncounted special authorities plus business firms and not-for-profit organizations that do the work of government on a contract basis.

There is diversity also in the means of controlling the margins of the American state. Executive and legislative branches of national and state governments have added control agents to their staffs. The separation of powers and executive-legislative rivalry mean that committee hearings of the legislature and bodies like the General Accounting Office, as well as the President's Office of Management and Budget, the Merit System Protection Board, cabinet departments, and the

Office of Contract Compliance take an interest in the margins. The media have developed investigative reporting to new levels of competence and interest.

Diversity and flexibility stand as the prime attractions of the special authorities and government contractors of the United States. Fortunate individuals and business firms can locate in communities on the basis of unique tax and service packages. Policy makers can tinker with the features of a special authority or a government contract in order to maximize any of several values: cost savings; managerial autonomy; community participation; or the racial, ethnic, and sex traits of the staff.

Diversity also creates negative features. In the United States, incoherence of structure and procedure plus uneven service provision and a fair amount of irresponsibility seem inevitable. There are so many units outside the control of major government officers. Added to this is the competition between federal, state, and local politicians, which minimizes the clarity of the directives that go out to the margins.

LESSONS FOR POLICY MAKERS AND REFORMERS

The growth of institutions on the margins of the modern state is not recent or temporary. It seems to be universal that modern states are welfare states and that they are driven by the weight of popular demand to create more programs than can be accommodated in core departments of government. The particulars of administrative units vary from one place to another, in response to underlying traits of each setting.

In the face of this reality is an ancient query of government: *Can agents of the state be subject to control, or held accountable for their actions?* Without an affirmative answer to this question, the state invites incoherence and disorder, and its legitimacy in the eyes of the population comes into question. Why pay taxes to a state that does not hold its officers accountable? Why accept regulations imposed by officers who claim to be acting in behalf of the state, but who may be acting in their own behalf?

To be sure, there is no clear evidence that problems are worse on the margins than at the core of the state. In each of the countries examined in this book it is possible to find administrative snafus, inefficiency, waste, and occasional corruption both in the traditional departments of government and in units placed on the margins of the state. Nevertheless, the problems coming from the margins raise a special question of legitimacy: Does the transfer of programs to the margins produce looser attitudes on the part of managers, who may have little fear of being held accountable?

Mechanisms exist to oversee the margins of these states and rein-in managers who go beyond the bounds of government policy. Yet controls are weak. Government officers in positions of control are overworked and tend to accept the value of managerial autonomy for the margins of the state. Many controls are cursory in operation. In the United States, agencies are routinely exempt from formal requirements to let contracts according to advertisements and competitive bidding. Australian control officers reveal a limited knowledge of the legislation meant to regulate their statutory authorities. The Israeli government has allowed some 120 companies owned by the municipalities to slip between the stools of two ministries (Finance and Interior) that should be overseeing them. Countless subsidiaries of Israeli government companies and their joint ventures are responsible, in practice, to no one beyond their own managers. Parliamentarians or executives in each of these countries have been embarrassed to find that they cannot even generate complete lists of bodies they have created on the margins of their states. Major problems may surface first in the mass media and come to the attention of government officials only after the media have exposed them.

Can officers of the state put their house in order? The question requires a consideration of the basic reasons for putting activities on the margins. Some of these reasons reveal a basic incapacity; the core departments of the government cannot handle all the activities demanded by citizens and promulgated by politicians. Other reasons for putting programs on the margins of the state reveal some measures of indifference or guile. Politicians respond to some demands out of political necessity, with little care about how the programs develop. If there is an available unit on the margin of the state, then it may handle the new program without great risk to the politician. If the program goes sour, the autonomy of the margin's administrators allows the government to avoid blame. Politicians put programs on the margins in order to keep their expenses off the government's budget, or to keep their employees off the civil service list. Politicians can thereby aid programs without violating—explicitly—public demands to limit the growth of government. Programs put on the margins are available to patronage demands from the politicians who create them: to hire a supporter outside the formal controls of the Civil Service Commission, or to provide service to a constituent whose case might not survive the scrutiny of a government office. It might be difficult to assign clear or simple motives to any one case of putting a program on the margins of the state; it is more important to recognize the variety of reasons for putting programs there. Each of these motives would stand in the way of a general reform that brought programs from the margins more clearly into the orbit of government control. It may not be so much a question of the state's inability to put its house in order as a lack of desire to give up the benefits received from having institutions on the margins, performing numerous important functions without close controls from the center.

The essence of being a politician is the ability to bear contrary pressures: to serve the people *and* to keep taxes low plus minimize government employment; to hire managers who can work quickly *and* to respect all the procedures for clearing major decisions with key government officers; to accept demands that the government hire people according to strict rules that respect competence, ethnicity, sex, or veteran status *and* allow some bodies to hire whomever they want. A typical way out of such conflicts is an ambiguous creation. The bodies on the margins of the state provide ideal conditions. The margins are *of*, but not *in*, the state. They promise the satisfaction of contrary demands and are essential to the political process in modern welfare states. The size of the margins reflects their popularity in government and implies that they cannot — or will not — be reformed by officials.

Is it possible to expect reforms to emerge from *outside the government* if we cannot expect systematic reform from official policy makers? Citizen involvement has been a common theme in efforts to make the welfare state more responsive. Political accountability may come not only through the conventional linkages between voters, elected officials, and the heads of administrative hierarchies but through the direct involvement of citizens in local service agencies. Citizens can also demand that government reform its own procedures in certain ways in order to make service agencies more coherent and responsive to clients, even without going so far as to include citizens within the policy process.

The prospect of reform from the outside seems unlikely to change in a basic way the profusion of agencies — either within core departments of government or on the margins of the state. Quite the contrary. Citizen demands seem likely to *increase* the number of actors in policy making and service delivery — and thus add to overall incoherence

—even while they remedy particular difficulties. Citizen boards that can advise, or even exercise controls over government contractors or special authorities may allow community input to a unit that has local impact. Seen from the perspective of general policy, however, such a citizen group becomes an additional choke-point that can hinder systemwide coordination or policy change.

Reforms designed with citizens in mind are catching on in many places. Although they do not aspire to general reform of the modern state, these reforms may render a state more effective and more responsive. The most common example is the ombudsman. This office is designed to aid the citizen who feels improperly treated by an agency. The ombudsman inquires into the merits of the claim, and if he feels it is justified, will bring the pressure of his recommendations against the errant agency. Depending on the jurisdiction, the ombudsman may deal with units on the margins of the state or may be limited to core departments of government. Generally, the ombudsman has no role in making service decisions per se. The role of ombudsman is an advisory one, but it is backed up with prestige and publicity that can be turned against officials who overlook its recommendations.

A weakness of the ombudsman role is that the ombudsman is a fixer of bad decisions. Many citizens have problems *prior* to being the target of bad decisions. For example, they do not know where to turn in the face of numerous service agencies, especially if their needs do not fit squarely into the orbit of one agency. A client who needs a combination of counseling, job training, medical treatment, and job placement may need to find and visit four separate agencies, yet he may not know where to begin. For this kind of problem, a multiple service referral agency (the Australians' "One-Stop Shop") is one answer. However, it must be conveniently located, widely advertised, and staffed by personnel who can solve the incoherent maze of agencies for clients.

It may be that no gimmick incorporated into the government can adequately serve the needs of citizens in an incoherent state. Perhaps only a private agent, working for a fee, will have an incentive to learn the shortest cuts through a service maze, and render advice that is truly in the interest of the client. There is an analog in the tax field, where private-sector lawyers or tax advisers sell information about court decisions that is more client serving than the advice purveyed by the tax agency itself. Another analog comes from the travel industry. Travel agents help their clients through a multiplicity of options offered by airlines and resorts that rivals the programs of government in their incoherence. In this case, the agents receive fees from the seller of travel services and not from the client directly.[1]

The model of the travel agent or the private tax adviser may be adapted to other sectors of public service. Storefront agencies can specialize in clusters of service that bridge the activities of several agencies in their locales. They would, in a sense, repackage the offerings of individual agencies to meet the needs of clients, sell advice as to which agencies a client should visit in which sequence, and actually fill out forms or accompany the client through the official maze. Payment for such service might come directly from the clients or via referral chits established by service agencies.

Payments to agents will, to be sure, raise questions of exploitation and corruption. Profit-making agents will position themselves between social service agencies and those citizen-clients who choose to pay something in order to enhance their prospects for good service. Undoubtedly some needy clients will pay more in agent fees than seems appropriate. Also, some clerks in the social service programs will accept favors in order to expedite the treatment of cases brought in by private agents. Similar problems occur in relations between other government offices and clients who employ attorneys or other intermediaries. Someone will have to worry about appropriate control procedures for the client's agent in the social service field. One can only hope that the controls will not be so oppressive as to offset any benefits entrepreneurial private agents can offer their clients.

Of course such a reform, like all other tinkering, will add one more bit to the general incoherence even while it lessens another incoherence. This seems to be the nature of reform possibilities. A general overhaul threatens too many interests. Incremental changes are feasible as gimmicks to fill in a chink in the service structure. Seldom do we see devices that can be prescribed for universal application. An administrative engineer must have detailed knowledge of the local terrain; this is an implicit message of comparative study.

There may be a general need for client-oriented services like the ombudsman, the referral unit, or even the private service agent. For reforms directed at linkages between government and units created on the margins of the state — to help the government control its margins — it seems necessary to take into account existing mechanisms and cultures. The margins of the Australian, Israeli, and American states are rooted in the underlying traits of each nation's most important experiences and institutions. There is no simple and obvious way to supervise or control the margins of the state. Sizable problems of management and lapses in political accountability seem endemic in the modern condition. Nevertheless, there are opportunities to alleviate them and lessen the harm they do.

Australia

An Australian policy maker might begin by simplifying and codifying the legislation that governs statutory authorities. The task of control units in the Treasury and other ministries would be easier if checkpoints for each statutory authority were similar (i.e., if each had to seek similar consultations or approvals for decisions involving similar sums of money). No obvious purpose is served — and the cost in incoherence is considerable — by requiring one authority to seek approval for an expenditure of $100,000 and allowing another authority to spend $150,000 or $200,000 merely by consulting with particular officers of the government. In a similar spirit the structures of authorities can be made uniform, with officers having similar titles responsible for similar internal procedures and relations with government officials. With small reforms of this kind, ministers and key administrative personnel would need to depend less on the managers of statutory authorities to guide them through unique and complex statutes.

At least in Victoria, ministers of the state government have ample statutory powers to involve themselves in the affairs of authorities. For the most part, they have chosen not to use their legal tools. They rely heavily on advice from their nominal subordinates in the authorities. When a matter of importance to state politics surfaces, it is the Premier, combining the functions of state Prime Minister and Minister of Finance, who engages the authority's managers. The simple device of simplifying and making uniform key features of each authority's statutes need not interfere with these accommodations among state politicians. If anything, reforms of the statutes will strengthen the Premier — and through him the political accountability of statutory authorities — by simplifying the task of professionals in the state Treasury to spot problems for their boss.

Israel

Israelis concerned with manageable reforms regarding the supervision and control over the margins of their state might improve central recordkeeping with respect to the companies, subsidiaries, and joint ventures subject to government control. The mechanism of the Authority for Government Companies already demonstrates a fair capacity for assembling policy-relevant information about government companies. But current legislation limits its jurisdiction to companies in which the government owns 50 percent of the shares. Out of its net are most joint ventures and subsidiaries. The information needed to begin expanded coverage exists in the Registry of Corporations, which lists the organizational structure and principal shareholders of all Israeli companies. No reformer would want to stifle the entrepreneurialism that is an exciting and productive feature of Israeli life. Nevertheless, with more thorough information about what it owns and controls, the government would be in a better position to comprehend and control what it is doing in economic allocations. A simple accumulation of information does not guarantee the replacement of incoherence with coherence, but the selective pursuit of information can bring some order to the policy-making sector that is now in the hands of ambitious and autonomous managers.

The United States

Anyone contemplating reforms for supervision and control over the margins of the American state must take account of the many special authorities and contractors, as well as the impressive number of control agents already in place. Numerous, often well-funded collectors of information are already employed by executive and legislative branches of the national government and many states. The idea of the ombudsman has caught on in many places. The media offer their own action-line services to compete with public offices in doing good for citizens. Investigative reporters look on a whiff of scandal as an entry to Pulitzer Prize competition and movement up the professional ladder. Organized groups of consumers, environmentalists, women, minorities, and others are alert to the possibility that special authorities or government contractors might violate requirements written for their benefit.

The prospect of exposure by public or private inquiry is not enough to keep the margins of the American state, as well as core departments of government, from serious problems. With the large number of control units adding to the problem of incoherence, it is not appropriate to suggest additional controllers. More in order would be better techniques of screening information from the margins, to increase the probability that problems will surface in a way that facilitates proper treatment. To deal with problems of irresponsible contracting, offices with responsibility for purchasing services might refine techniques of comparing contracting costs with the costs of in-house activities. The national government has recently examined its policy on contracting and has added more explicit comparative cost criteria to that policy. Such techniques could be enhanced to deal with issues of service quality as well as cost differential. Contracting costs are often cheaper than those of government departments simply because lower-quality services are offered, or initial wage bills are sharply lower, or low profits are estimated in a period of "introductory free offer." Governments might consider contracts for longer terms, with stronger assurances of service quality and price stability.

The Modesty of Proposals

In our continuing effort to tidy up the margins of the state, we should recall Australia's experience with rabbits and blackberries. Mechanisms that work well in one society may produce chaos elsewhere. It would be lovely to combine the good order, high service quality, and explicit policy controls of Australia's statutory authorities with some of the entrepreneurialism that vibrates on the margins of the Israeli and American states. But think of the chaos wrought by such an innocent transplant! Aggressive entrepreneurs could perform administrative rape on the few central-control personnel in Australian governments, who expect managers of statutory authorities to comply with their statutes. The fellow who departed from the conventional view of law (i.e., do only what is explicitly permitted) to something more akin to the Israeli or American version (i.e., do anything not explicitly prohibited) could have a field day — at least until the government got around to establishing a formal commission of inquiry.

The Australian statutes score high on political accountability — they are explicit and subject to parliamentary and public scrutiny — but work well only in a cultural setting of compliance. Where avoidance of control is a popular norm, as in the more individualistic and aggressive societies of Israel and the United States, detailed law only adds to the complexity of government. Incoherence is likely to prevail over control, as explicit law provides temporary delusion for controllers while the entrepreneurs learn to hide the tracks of their evasions.

A Transplant That Might Be Helpful

To be careful about cross-national transplants does not mean to shun them altogether! Some lessons for Australia and the United States may come from Israel's Authority for Government Companies. An Australian version, labeled an Authority for Statutory Authorities, could be located in the Prime Minister's Department or in the Commonwealth Finance Ministry, or could be attached to state government treasuries. In the United States, an Authority for Government Contractors could be put in a prominent place at national, state, and local governments. In state governments it might be attached to the Governor's Office and given the following powers, patterned closely after the Israeli model:

1. Advise the chief executive on matters related to government contracting

2. In accordance with directives from the chief executive, deal with matters common to all government contractors or to particular classes of them

3. Keep track of, and assist in, the implementation of the government auditor's recommendations relating to government contractors

4. Advise and assist government contractors in the conduct of their business

5. Report on the activities of government contractors, the implementation of their contracts, their costs, and their policies with respect to personnel

6. Examine the reports of government contractors and the material on which they are based and make comments on them to the contractors and the chief executive

7. Assist in the establishment and termination of government contracts, as well as in the compromise settlements and arrangements thereof

8. Carry out, with respect to government contractors, any function entrusted to it by the chief executive

These add up to impressive powers, which are open to the imagination and strength of the authority's director. In addressing the needs of policy makers regarding contractors (or, in the case of Australia, statutory authorities), it is necessary to wrestle with the dilemma of autonomy and accountability. Policy makers may require a greater capacity to comprehend and control units on the margins of their state. However, they should not pursue the virtues of central control so thoroughly as to override the virtues of creating marginal units in the first place. Neither should central officials overload themselves with a mass of routine supervision so that their oversight activities must become indiscriminate because of the work volume.

What emerges from this set of constraints is an Authority for Government Contractors that should rely on existing government agencies for routine controls but that has a combination of legal authority, administrative resources, and a sensitivity to the important analyses not being done by the organization already in place. The director should establish boundaries between the authority's functions and those of other oversight bodies. Details would depend on conditions in each setting. Examples of such accommodations are

Reliance on departments of government for the routine review of their contractors' compliance with written agreements, and reliance on the government auditor to check this as part of its periodic review of each department

Reliance on the public prosecutor to deal with violations that invite criminal proceedings

Reliance on legislators and their committees, the ombudsman, or other citizen-oriented units for primary response to clients who complain that contractor-run programs do not offer proper services.

The Authority for Government Contractors should husband its resources for data collection and analyses not pursued by other units. Its major tangible accomplishment could be

An annual report showing the extent of contracting by each department of government, specifying such items as the dollar value of contracts; the number of full-time-equivalent personnel on the payroll of contractors; instances of formal complaints with respect to contractors' lack of compliance with written agreements; plus results of each department's efforts to assess the quality of its contractors' activities

The benefits of such a report will include the activities it prompts among government departments and auditors to be more diligent in their own oversight of contractors. Most of the authority director's time might be spent educating other government officials about important issues of management and accountability that touch on contracting. The primary responsibility for routine oversight must remain with the departments that arrange contracts. Nevertheless, this could be done in a way that the chief executive and other elected officials keep in touch with contracted activities that hitherto have been on the margins of their awareness.

LESSONS FOR POLITICAL SCIENCE

Political scientists have much to learn from the margins of the state. Some may not want to recognize what is happening. With massive resources allocated by units on the margins of the state — effectively independent from core institutions of legislative, executive, and major administrative departments — much of political science teeters on the brink of obsolescence. The minutiae of electoral strategy and legislative wrangling have less and less to do with who rules and who gets what in a modern state.

"Crisis" is a cheap slogan in a world of many aspirations. Nevertheless, ignorance about the margins of the state qualifies as a crisis among the people charged with understanding the state. The responsibility for such a crisis can be spread widely, among government officials, journalists, and active citizens as well as among political scientists. As scholar-specialists in affairs of the state, however, political scientists carry more than the average burden of repairing this ignorance about its margins.

Academic departments of political science and public administration can add courses in "public enterprise" alongside traditional offerings in administration and policy making. Materials about public enterprise in all its forms — including authorities, contractors, government companies — should find a place within existing courses dealing with public policy and administration. Political scientists who specialize in public opinion, voting, parties, interest groups, courts, legislatures, chief executives, or politics generally in the United States or other countries should not drop everything in behalf of this call. Ideally, traditional processes and institutions will remain central to the political fray and the allocation of public resources. Yet traditional processes and institutions are not alone. They have welcomed new actors in public enterprises, and granted them important places on the margins of all states. Unless students know about these entities, they will recognize only part of what is politics.

Programs of instruction are valuable not only in their own right but for the further inquiries they provoke. The topics of research extend from the simple to the profound. There is no hard information in many countries about the basic characteristics of the margins, in terms of money collected or spent, number of people employed, or even institutions that exist. The job may be too great and too fluid for the resources of a scholar; occasional commissions of government or legislative committees have failed at such tasks. But scholars can press for recordkeeping to be done in a centralized and systematic manner. Without this basic information, research into the quality of activities on the margins of the state can be done only episodically. Case studies make acceptable demonstrations of things that happen, but they cannot claim to represent important trends without substantial knowledge of the larger population from which they come. The annual reports of Australian Authorities for Statutory Authorities or American Authorities for Government Contractors—should they come to be— will boost the quality of scholarship, as well as the quality of government control over bodies on the margins of the states.

Political scientists should pursue the same questions about the margins of the state that they pursue about conventional government: *Who rules?* and *Who gets what?* There is a need for internal studies of special authorities, contractors, and government companies, as well as studies of the services they provide to clients and the linkages between the margins and the core of government. The essence of marginality puts stress on issues of political accountability and mechanisms that link—or fail to link—activities on the margins with the government officials who are supposed to decide about public policy. This book has tried to arouse interest on the general topic of the margins of the state and the specific topic of national variations. It has concentrated mostly on issues of management and accountability within this framework.

This book has stressed the value of cross-national comparison in exposing important features on the margins of the state. Bodies on the margins of Australia, Israel, and the United States differ from one another most clearly in their legal formats, but they diverge also on styles of management and traits of accountability. Only occasionally did the chapters on each country allude to internal variations. Yet the value of comparison should extend to subnational research. The states of the United States differ sharply among themselves on a number of social, economic, and political traits. Other research has found these differences mirrored in the public policies promulgated by state and local governments. These same governments seem likely to differ in their general policies toward contracting, as well as in the character of work done by contractors. Other insights might come from systematic comparisons of the statutory authorities attached to different jurisdictions in Australia, or of companies attached to different ministries of the Israeli government.

Is it possible to generalize at this point about the prominent actors that determine *Who Rules?* or *Who Gets What?* The findings from Australia, Israel, and the United States indicate that managers dominate the margins of the state. More tricky is the designation of government officers who involve themselves effectively in supervision and control. Occasionally, elected officials look to units on the margins for matters of great political moment or for chores they would not ask of a government department. To know which government administrators deal with units on the margin, it is necessary to look at each setting. In Victoria it is senior officials of the state Treasury, and occasionally the permanent head of a department. Interesting figures in Israel are civil servants who double as government representatives on a company's board of directors and ministry officials responsible for reviewing the company's requests. Americans who bear scrutiny are national, state, and local administrators who negotiate contracts with vendors and personnel in budget or procurement agencies who review contracts for formal approval. With respect to special authorities in the United States, key actors are banks, insurance companies, and underwriters who set the terms of borrowing and service provision.

More than the details of policy making and service delivery should attract the attention of political scientists to the margins of the state. The concept of the state plus the conventional mechanisms of democracy bear examination. This is true not only for concerns about the margins of the state described in this book.

The definition of the margins of the state may stretch beyond the units considered here. Multinational corporations also challenge conventional notions of the state. Multinationals wield enough power to challenge the sovereignty of states — both in their wealthy "homelands" and in the poor countries that view them as outlanders.[2]

The experiences of great and small governments with the multinational oil companies suggest that these commercial giants have no homeland, and little sense of being subordinate to any sovereign outside of themselves. Formal government inquiries into company records have stumbled against ambiguous reports or assertions of privacy — whether the inquiries deal with the amount of petroleum available, company policies on pricing, or the accounting procedures used to determine profits and taxes.

Subsequent studies about multinationals and units on the margins of states may put them in the same category of what has been the terrain of government officials and political science. The modern state is more than the core departments of government. Bodies described in this book as being on the margins are one competitor of government; multinationals are another. Each coopts and constrains government officials, and comes to speak for the government implicitly if not explicitly.

Multinationals and bodies on the margins of the state also resemble one another in assertions of autonomy from the state, and in a disinclination to report clearly details about their size or activity. Much that is written about them is conjecture, and is tinged with myth. Moreover, neither multinationals nor bodies on the margins of the state can be purged without threatening great change and — at the least — inconvenience to both citizens and policy makers. It seems to be in the nature of multinationals and marginal bodies that they are inevitable and vexing. That they are largely opaque to political science is part of the discomfort associated with them.

The margins of the modern state are broad and complex. Unless we as political scientists deal seriously with them, we cannot claim to be comprehensive with respect to politics or public policy. A wit might label this book a trumpet in behalf of marginalia. That may be true. Nevertheless, the organizations that have grown up on the margins of the state are no trivial concern to us as citizens, scholars, or policy makers.

For a political scientist concerned with the margins of the state, the query, *Accountability to whom?* is critical. Perspectives vary with the interests involved. To officials of the core government, accountability may entail linkages of control from the center to the margins, and full reports from the margins to the center. Managers who work on the margins have their own ideas about accountability. They value control of their own organizations and claim autonomy from the center of government. Employees may cite their claims of professionalism and seek independence from their administrative superiors. Clients have their interests, too, and may identify community control as the focus of accountability. For the political scientist, there is no simple choice among such contending claims. Each has formulas to justify its own brand of accountability. It is more certain that actors who claim control may not in fact exercise control. The proliferation of bodies on the margins of the state challenges both the political scientist who wants to know *Who does rule?* as well as the political scientist who wants to judge *Who should rule?*

The question of *Who rules?* is related to another question of great interest to political scientists: *Why don't programs work?* This is the issue of *implementation*. The topic has long been implicit in research about public policy, but has received sharper focus with the publication of books like *Implementation* by Jeffrey Pressman and Aaron Wildavsky and *The Implementation Game* by Eugene Bardach. The literature indicates that many problems stand in the way of carrying out program goals. One problem is the complexity of organizations. If policy makers and administrators do not know how to motivate or control the organizations of the state, they cannot predict the outputs that will result from their programs. With numerous bodies on the margins of the state, the problem is more severe. Each body on the margins may claim a degree of autonomy from officers of the state. The implementation of job training in the United States, for example, depends on countless contractors who take part in program design and service delivery at national, state, and local levels. Even to learn what is happening, government officers contract with other firms to do program evaluation. With claims of autonomy at each stage, there are countless opportunities for snafu, mismanagement, or irresponsibility. Under such conditions, the appropriate question for the margins of the state may not be *Who rules?* but *Does anybody rule?*

Notes

Chapter 1. The Incoherence of Welfare States

1. Annmarie Hauck Walsh, *The Public's Business: The Politics and Practices of Government Corporations* (Cambridge, Mass.: MIT Press, 1978), p. 6.

2. Abraham Daniel, *Labor Enterprises in Israel* (Jerusalem: Jerusalem Academic Press, 1976), 2:126.

3. D. C. Hague, W. J. M. MacKenzie, and A. Barker, *Public Policy and Private Interests* (London: Macmillan, 1975); and *Melbourne Age*, 3 January 1979.

4. William Taubman, *Governing Soviet Cities: Bureaucratic Politics and Urban Development in the USSR* (New York: Praeger, 1973).

5. Jacek Tarkowski, "Decision-Making in the Polish Local Political System," in *Local Politics, Development and Participation: A Cross-National Study of Interrelationships*, ed. F. C. Bruhns, F. Cazzola, and J. Wiatre (Pittsburgh: University Center for International Studies, 1974).

6. Daniel Guttman and Barry Willner, *The Shadow Government: The Government's Multi-Billion-Dollar Giveaway of Its Decision-Making Powers to Private Management Consultants, "Experts," and Think Tanks* (New York: Pantheon, 1976); and John D. Hanrahan, *Government for Sale: Contracting-Out the New Patronage* (Washington, D.C.: American Federation of State, County, and Municipal Employees, 1977).

7. I am indebted to Professor Peter Self of the London School of Economics, who suggested the image of the pyramids in conversation, and to Professor

David Corbett of Flinders University, Adelaide, South Australia, who suggested the role of private agents as contractors to aid the citizen through the incoherence of the state.

8. Mike Royko, *Boss* (New York: Signet, 1971).

9. Robert A. Caro, *The Power Broker: Robert Moses and the Fall of New York* (New York: Knopf, 1974).

10. For examples of the voluminous research on different sides of political versus nonpolitical influences on state and local policies, see Herbert Jacob and Kenneth N. Vines, eds., *Politics in the American States* (2nd ed.; Boston: Little Brown, 1971).

11. Fred W. Riggs, *Administration in Developing Countries: The Theory of Prismatic Society* (Boston: Houghton Mifflin, 1964).

12. Michael H. Best and William E. Connolly, *The Politicized Economy* (Lexington, Mass.: Heath, 1976).

13. Thomas S. Kuhn, *The Structures of Scientific Revolutions* (Chicago: University of Chicago Press, 1962).

14. See, for example, Bruce L. R. Smith and D. C. Hague, eds., *The Dilemma of Accountability in Modern Government: Independence versus Control* (London: Macmillan, 1971); David Coombes, *State Enterprise: Business or Politics?* (London: George Allen, 1971); Hans Calmfors, Francine F. Rabinowitz, and Daniel J. Alesch, *Urban Government for Greater Stockholm: A Study of Policy Development* (New York: Praeger, 1968); Francesco Kjellberg, *Municipal Decentralization: A Framework for the Study of Neighborhood Government* (Oslo: Institute of Political Science, University of Oslo, 1976); Richard Rose and Guy Peters, "The Political Consequences of Economic Overload: On the Possibility of Political Bankruptcy" (paper presented at the annual meeting of the American Political Science Association, Washington, D.C., 1977); Ghita Ionescu, *Centripetal Politics: Government and the New Centres of Power* (London: Hart-Davis, MacGibbon, 1975); R. Kelf-Cohen, *Twenty Years of Nationalization: The British Experience* (London: Macmillan, 1969); Stuart Holland, ed., *The State as Entrepreneur: New Dimensions for Public Enterprise: The IRI State Shareholding Formula* (London: Weidenfeld and Nicolson, 1972); W. Friedmann and J. F. Garner, eds., *Government Enterprise: A Comparative Study* (London: Stevens, 1970); Hague, MacKenzie, and Barker, *Public Policy and Private Interests*; plus the numerous books and articles cited in chapters 2–4 on Australia, Israel, and the United States.

15. Vincent Ostrom, *The Intellectual Crisis in American Public Administration* (University, Ala.: University of Alabama Press, 1974).

16. Larry B. Hill, "Institutionalization, the Ombudsman, and Bureaucracy," *American Political Science Review* 68 (September 1974): 1075–85; and Nathalie Marguerite Kerber, *The Israeli Ombudsman* (Jerusalem: State Comptroller, 1976).

Chapter 2. Australia: Statutory Authorities and Law-Abiding Managers

1. Donald Horne, *The Lucky Country: Australia Today* (Baltimore: Penguin, 1964).

2. By way of comparison, Americans with $32,000 of taxable income, filing jointly, pay a marginal rate of 39 percent for U.S. individual income tax. References to Australian currency are given in Australian dollars. All other dollar figures used in the book are U.S. dollars.

3. Australian Senate, Standing Committee on Finance and Government Operations, "Progress Report," September 1977. Mimeo.

4. *Australian*, 6 January 1979.

5. R. W. Eggleston, *State Socialism in Victoria* (London: King, 1932), pp. 27–28. Other general works on statutory authorities include R. L. Wettenhall, "Government Department of Statutory Authority?" *Public Administration* (Australia) 27 (December 1968): 350-59; Leon Peres, "The Resurrection of Autonomy," *Public Administration* (Australia) 27 (December 1969): 360–70; John C. Pickett, *Public Authorities and Development in Melbourne* (Canberra: Urban Research Unit, Australian National University, 1973).

6. *Victoria Yearbook, 1975* (Melbourne: Government Printer, 1976), p. 133.

7. Marian Simms, "Ideology, Rhetoric and Liberal Party Policies on Public Enterprises" (paper presented at the Australiasian Political Studies Association Conference, August 1977). Mimeo.

8. A. F. Davies, "The Government of Victoria," in *The Government of the Australian States*, ed. S. R. Davis (Melbourne: Longman, 1960), p. 190.

9. Jean Holmes, "Political Chronicle-Victoria," University of Melbourne, Department of Political Science, February 1978. Mimeo.

10. Michael Cannon, *The Land Boomers* (Melbourne: Melbourne University Press, 1966).

11. State of Victoria, *Report of the Board of Inquiry into Certain Land Purchases of the Housing Commission and Questions Arising Therefrom* (Melbourne: Government Printer, March 1978).

12. See, for example, Herbert Jacob and Kenneth N. Vines, *Politics in the American States* (2nd ed.; Boston: Little, Brown, 1971).

13. Cecil Edwards, *Brown Power: A Jubilee History of the State Electricity Commission of Victoria* (Melbourne: State Electricity Commission of Victoria, 1969).

14. Campbell Sharman, *The Premier's Conference: An Essay in Federal State Interaction* (Canberra: Australian National University Department of Political Science, 1977); and Patrick Weller and James Cutt, *Treasury Control in Australia* (Sydney: Ian Novak, 1976).

15. As elsewhere in this book, the term "state" is used in its generic sense. In the case of Australia, it refers to the "state" of both the Commonwealth and state governments.

16. The origin of the quotation is Sir Arthur Street, as provided in R. L. Wettenhall, *A Guide to Tasmanian Government Administration* (Hobart: Platypus, 1968), p. 3.

17. Martyn Forrest, "The Organization of Government in Western Australia," University of Western Australia, Department of Political Science, 1977, p. 29. Mimeo.

18. Ibid.

19. Ibid., pp. 33–35.

20. Australian Senate, Standing Committee on Finance and Government Operations.

21. For similar comment with respect to the United States, see Annmarie Hauck Walsh, *The Public's Business: The Politics and Practices of Government Corporations* (Cambridge, Mass.: MIT Press, 1978), chaps. 7–8.

22. Elmer B. Staats, "New Problems of Accountability for Federal Programs," in *The New Political Economy: The Public Use of the Private Sector*, ed. Bruce L. R. Smith (London: Macmillan, 1975).

23. Edwards, *Brown Power*.

24. Stanley Brogden, *Australia's Two-Airline Policy* (Melbourne: Melbourne University Press, 1968); and David Corbett, *Politics and the Airlines* (London: George Allen and Unwin, 1965).

25. Jean Holmes, *The Government of Victoria* (St. Lucia: University of Queensland Press, 1976).

26. I am indebted to Roger L. Wettenhall, C. Ross Curnow, and Jean Holmes for comments to this point.

27. Eggleston, *State Socialism in Victoria*.

28. Richard Neustadt, *Presidential Power: The Politics of Leadership* (New York: Wiley, 1960).

29. Davies, "The Government of Victoria."

30. J. C. Trethowan, "Public Enterprise," *Australian Journal of Public Administration* 36, no. 1 (March 1977): 44–51.

31. Jean Holmes, "Administrative Style and Sir John Monash," *Public Administration* (Australia) 29 (September 1970): 233 ff. A more complete work is Jean Holmes, "The State Electricity Commission of Victoria: A Case Study in Autonomy" (master's thesis, University of Melbourne, 1969).

32. Cannon, *The Land Boomers*.

3. Israel: Entrepreneurial Managers on the Margins

1. *Annual Report No. 24* (Jerusalem: State Comptroller, 1974), pp. 900–923. In Hebrew.

2. *Report on the Audit of the Government Company for Coins and Medals, Ltd.* (Jerusalem: State Comptroller, 1975). In Hebrew.

3. Abraham Daniel, *Labor Enterprises in Israel* (Jerusalem: Jerusalem Academic Press, 1976), 2:126.

4. Ibid., p. 160.

5. Ibid., p. 182.

6. G. Sheffer and Y. Manor, "Planning in Fund-Raising for Israel," The Hebrew University Department of Political Science, Jerusalem, 1976. Mimeo.

7. Joseph Douer, *State Audit of Government Corporations in Israel* (Jerusalem: State Comptroller, 1973), chap. 2.

8. Gerald E. Caiden, *Israel's Administrative Culture* (Berkeley: University of California Institute of Government Studies, 1970).

9. Ira Sharkansky, "How to Cope with the Bureaucracy," *Jerusalem Quarterly* 6 (Winter 1978): 80–93.

10. Larry Hill, "Bureaucracy, the Bureaucratic Auditor, and the Ombudsman: An Ideal Type Analysis," in *State Audit: Developments in Public Accountability*, ed. Yehezkel Dror (forthcoming).

11. *Annual Report No. 5* (Jerusalem: Ombudsman, 1976). In Hebrew.

12. *Report on Government Companies and Government Share Investment* (Jerusalem: Treasury, 1977), p. v. In Hebrew.

13. This section relies on Ira Sharkansky, "Control at the Margins of Government: The State Comptroller and the Public Corporations of Israel," in Dror, ed., *State Audit*.

14. Douer, *State Audit of Government Corporations in Israel*, chap. 5.

15. *Selected Findings on Matters of Principle* (Jerusalem: State Comptroller, 1976); and *Norms for Public Administration* (Jerusalem: State Comptroller, 1969).

16. *Organization and Administration of Public Enterprises: Selected Papers* (New York: United Nations Department of Economic and Social Affairs, 1968); *Organization, Management and Supervision of Public Enterprises in Developing Countries* (New York: United Nations Department of Economic and Social Affairs, 1973).

17. *Report on the Audit of the Government Company for Coins and Medals* (Jerusalem: State Comptroller, 1976). In Hebrew.

18. *Report on Audit of Israel Aviation Industry, Ltd.* (Jerusalem: State Comptroller, 1976). In Hebrew.

19. *Report on Audit of "Amidar": The National Company to House Immigrants in Israel, Ltd.* (Jerusalem: State Comptroller, 1975). In Hebrew.

4. The United States: Special Authorities and Contracting

1. John D. Hanrahan, *Government for Sale: Contracting-Out the New Patronage* (Washington, D.C.: American Federation of State, County, and Municipal Employees, 1977), p. 217.

2. Ibid., p. 218.

3. U.S. House of Representatives, Committee on Post Office and Civil Service, *Contracting Out of Jobs and Services* (Washington, D.C.: U.S. Government Printing Office, 1977), p. 31

4. Daniel Guttman and Barry Willner, *The Shadow of Government: The Government's Multi-Billion-Dollar Giveaway of Its Decision-Making Powers to Private Management Consultants, "Experts," and Think Tanks* (New York: Pantheon, 1976), pp. 152, 189.

5. Annmarie Hauck Walsh, *The Public's Business: The Politics and Practices of Government Corporations* (Cambridge, Mass.: MIT Press, 1978), p. 6.

6. See Neil Gilbert, "The Transformation of Social Services," *Social Service Review* 51 (December 1977): 624–41.

7. Elma Phillipson Cole, "Voluntary Agencies in the Purchase of Care and Services," in *Purchase of Care and Services in the Health and Welfare Fields*, ed. Iris R. Winogrond (Milwaukee: University of Wisconsin-Milwaukee School of Social Welfare, 1970).

8. U.S. House of Representatives, *Contracting Out of Jobs and Services*, pp. 43–44.

9. Ibid., p. 2.

10. Walsh, *The Public's Business*, pp. 162–63.

11. Eleanor L. Brilliant, "Private or Public: A Model of Ambiguities," *Social Service Review* 47 (September 1973): 384–96.

12. P. Nelson Reid, "Reforming the Social Services Monopoly," *Social Work* 17 (November 1972): 44–54.

13. Brilliant, "Private or Public"; see also Ralph M. Kramer, "Voluntary Agencies and the Use of Public Funds: Some Policy Issues," *Social Service Review* 40 (November 1966): 15–26; and Gordon Manser, "Further Thoughts on Purchase of Service," *Social Casework* 55 (July 1974): 421–27.

14. *Wall Street Journal*, 24 and 25 January 1979.

15. David W. Young, "Referral and Placement in Child Care: The New York Purchase-of-Service System," *Public Policy* 22 (Summer 1974): 293–328.

16. George Wiley, "Advocacy for the Poor," in Winogrond, ed., *Purchase of Care and Services*.

17. Guttman and Willner, *The Shadow of Government*, p. 201.

18. "Community Human Services Project," Wisconsin Department of Health and Social Services, undated. Mimeo.

19. "Survey for Assessing the Needs of Community Services Boards (51/42/437 Boards) and Evaluating the Needs Servicing Capabilities of the Division of

Mental Hygiene," Laufenberg Research and Development Institute, Chippewa Falls, Wisc., 1977. Mimeo.

20. As in the case of Australia and Israel, there is a difference between the meaning of "State" and "state." Here the "margins of the American state" refers to the generic concept, including bodies on the margins of U.S. national, state, and local governments.

21. Robert L. Lineberry and Ira Sharkansky, *Urban Politics and Public Policy* (New York: Harper, 1978); and Ira Sharkansky, *The United States: A Study of a Developing Country* (New York: Longman, 1975).

22. Vincent Ostrom, *The Intellectual Crisis in American Public Administration* (University, Ala.: University of Alabama Press, 1974).

23. Guttman and Willner, *The Shadow of Government*, p. 26.

24. Hanrahan, *Government for Sale*, p. 69.

25. U.S. House of Representatives, *Contracting Out Jobs and Services*, pp. 67–68.

26. Ibid., p. 21.

27. Hanrahan, *Government for Sale*, pp. 3–4.

28. Guttman and Willner, *The Shadow of Government*, pp. 55–56, 120, 151.

29. Martha Derthick, *Uncontrollable Spending for Social Services Grants* (Washington, D.C.: Brookings Institution, 1975).

30. Hanrahan, *Government for Sale*, pp. 143–44.

31. The material on Robert Moses comes from Robert A. Caro, *The Power Broker: Robert Moses and the Fall of New York City* (New York: Knopf, 1974).

32. Walsh, *The Public's Business*, pp. 234–55.

33. Ibid., p. 87.

34. The State of Wisconsin, Joint Committee for Review of Administrative Rules, correspondence, 18 July 1978.

35. Wisconsin Department of Health and Social Services, memorandum dated 11 July 1978.

36. U.S. House of Representatives, *Contracting Out Jobs and Services*, pp. 2–16.

37. Ibid., p. 22.

38. "Survey for Assessing the Needs," p. 50.

39. Wisconsin Department of Health and Social Services, Bureau of Planning and Analysis, *Assessment of the Division of Correction Purchase of Service Program* (Madison: Wisconsin Department of Health and Social Services, June 1977).

40. AFSCME Council 24, Wisconsin State Employees Union, correspondence, 12 July 1978.

41. Government Employees Council, AFL-CIO, "Presentation of the Government Employees Council, AFL-CIO, to the Executive Branch in Reference

to Bureau of the Budget Bulletin 60-2," Washington, 1962. See also Gilbert, "The Transformation of Social Services."

42. Michael D. Reagan, *Politics, Economics and the General Welfare* (Chicago: Scott Foresman, 1965), chap. 5.

43. U.S. Office of Management and Budget, "Statement by the Honorable Lester A. Fettig, Administrator for Federal Procurement Policy, Office of Management and Budget, Before the Subcommittee on Research and Development of the House Armed Services Committee, April 10, 1978," p. 3. Mimeo.

44. U.S. Office of Management and Budget, circular dated 24 August 1976. Mimeo.

45. U.S. Office of Management and Budget, "Statement by the Honorable Lester A. Fettig," p. 4.

46. This section relies on Walsh, *The Public's Business*, esp. chaps. 8 and 10.

47. Ibid., pp. 267 ff.; see also Robert H. Connery and Gerald Benjamin, *Rockefeller of New York: Executive Power in the Statehouse* (Ithaca, N.Y.: Cornell University Press, 1979).

Chapter 5. Lessons from the Margins of the State

1. My thanks are due to Professor David Corbett of Flinders University in Adelaide, South Australia, for suggesting the mechanism of the private agent.

2. See, for example, Raymond Vernon, *Storm Over the Multinationals: The Real Issues* (Cambridge, Mass.: Harvard University Press, 1977)

Index